WRITING TO LIVE

If we want to live in a world that is fair, we have to make sure that the literacies we enact in our classrooms can contribute to a just world. If we want to live in a world of freedom, then our students must learn how to communicate and reason as free people.

From "Dimensions of Writing the World:
Looking at Critical Composing from Three Directions," by Randy Bomer

WRITING TO LIVE
How to Teach Writing for Today's World

Lorraine Wilson

HEINEMANN
Portsmouth, NH

Heinemann
A division of Reed Elsevier Inc.
361 Hanover Street
Portsmouth, NH 03801–3912
www.heinemann.com

Offices and agents throughout the world

Library of Congress Cataloging-in-Publication Data
Wilson, Lorraine.
  Writing to live : how to teach writing for today's world / Lorraine Wilson.
    p. cm.
  Includes bibliographical references.
  ISBN 0-325-00837-X (alk. paper)
  1. Creative writing (Elementary education).   2. Critical pedagogy.   I. Title.
LB1576.W48882 2006
372.62'3—dc22   2005021109

Editor: Danny Miller
Production: Elizabeth Valway
Cover design: Linda Knowles
Cover photography: Jaqueline Hendrey
Composition: House of Equations, Inc.
Manufacturing: Louise Richardson

Printed in the United States of America on acid-free paper
10   09   08   07   06   RRD   1   2   3   4   5

CONTENTS

FOREWORD

Archimedes is given credit for coining the expression "Eureka, I understand." History tells us that, after putting much cognitive effort into trying to understand the conceptual complexities associated with what we now know to be the principles of specific gravity, he decided to take a bath. As the water ran over his body and began to fill the tub, the complexities of what he'd been trying to understand fell into place, the principle of specific gravity came to him, and he shouted, "Eureka, I understand!"

Like everyone who has vital interests in, and commitments to, education, I'm continually striving for similar moments of clarity. Unfortunately, they seem to be getting fewer and farther between, so when I have one, it is a memorable event.

I recently had one. Unlike Archimedes, I was not in the bath but sitting at my desk. Rather than thinking about the complexities of physics and mathematics, I'd just finished reading *Writing to Live*. Instead of shouting, like Archimedes, a quiet voice in my head paraphrased him thus:

> Now I get it! Now I can see how it's possible to take the new knowledge, information, and theories about language, learning, and pedagogy—that have impacted on the field of writing in the last decade or so—link with the best of the "old" knowledge developed in the 1970s and 1980s, and construct a coherent pedagogy of writing for the twenty-first century. This book has the potential to reframe and revitalize the teaching of writing!

What is it about this book that turned it into an "Archimedes moment" for me? I think it has something to do with the consequences of what Richard Wurman has identified as "information anxiety" (Wurman 1989, 2000). Let me explain.

For at least two decades now researchers and theory builders have been creating new information about literacy, language, and learning at an exponential rate. Literacy educators, from kindergarten teachers to preservice teacher-education professors (like me), have been under constant pressure to make sense of this explosion of information and somehow apply it to the educational settings in which we operate.

Not only are some of us overwhelmed by this avalanche of information, many of us are confused by the multiplicity of conflicting claims and counterclaims that have emerged from the plethora of competing points of view.

When it comes to the teaching of reading or writing, these conflicting points of view have enjoyed wide dissemination and discussion in professional journals, the popular media, and government inquiries. The confusion is compounded when punitive regimes of accountability based on standardized tests are added to the mix. Unfortunately, many of us are so overwhelmed by all this information, or so concerned with ensuring that our students "pass the tests," that we sometimes resort to simplistic commercial quick fixes or formulaic, mind-numbing, lockstep approaches developed by educational entrepreneurs. For many of us, this is the only way to feel secure that we are covering the syllabus.

There are two serious consequences of this kind of information anxiety. One is that teachers are professionally de-skilled. They come to rely on quick fix, formulaic approaches being peddled by publishers and other educational entrepreneurs. The other is a retreat from the learner-centered constructivist pedagogies of the '70s and '80s that revolutionized the teaching of writing. Often this retreat is accompanied by a regression to the teacher-centered, behaviorist educational ideologies of a previous age.

A little history might clarify what I'm trying to communicate. During the 1950s (when I began my teaching career), education theory in Australia was dominated by behaviorist psychology with its inherent rationalistic philosophies regarding language and the structure of knowledge. Things were much the same in the United States (Edelsky 1999). This dominance continued well into the 1960s. It was a time when language was considered to be a hierarchical set of propositions and relationships that could be reduced to a finite set of discrete hierarchical units. This was particularly true for the written form of language. Because I had been imbued with the same dominant behaviorist ideology in my preservice teacher education program, I taught writing as a finite set of macroskills, which, in turn, could be broken down into subskills that once mastered gave the learner control of the overall systems that made it up. Furthermore, I taught these skills independently of each other. Although I wasn't consciously aware of it, in those days I treated learners as the proverbial empty vessels that needed to be filled with imperial gallons of linguistic fact. During composition lessons (i.e., "written expression") I treated my students as passive recipients and expected them to master the skills of effective writing by learning rules and by engaging in repetitive drills of subskills. I found teaching writing in those days to be relatively simple and easy. As long as I adhered to the formulaic underpinnings of behaviorist ideology, the principals and administrators to whom I was accountable considered me to be "doing a good job in the teaching of writing." It was also comforting to attribute the failure of my methods to some kind of deficit or flaw in the genetic or cultural backgrounds of those who didn't learn to write clearly and effectively.

By the end of the 1970s, traditional views of language and literacy acquisition were challenged by linguistic, psycholinguistic and sociolinguistic research that refuted much of the behaviorist ideology that had dominated the pedagogy of writing. The 1980s were characterized by so-called new approaches to the teaching of literacy. A new focus on the needs of the individual emerged. A new emphasis on meaning, social context, the links between modes of language, and the overall cognitive development of the learner began to influence the development of new theories of literacy education. These new emphases culminated in Donald Graves' conceptualization of writing as a process rather than a product. Graves argued that writing should not be seen as something to be produced once a week in composition classes, but rather as a process of composing meaning. Graves identified the dangers inherent in adhering to prescriptive approaches to writing, particularly with young children. He coined the term *Process Writing* and summed up the beginnings of the approach during an early trip to Australia:

> Children want to write. For years we have underestimated their urge to make marks on paper. We have underestimated that urge because of a lack of understanding of the writing process. Our research has established that all children can write at 5–6 years old, can enjoy doing so, and can make at this time some of the most rapid and delightful growth in writing of their entire lives. We should look at the system which imposes meaningless topics and not at the children for the reasons why so many are turned off writing. . . . When people own a place, they look after it; but when it belongs to someone else, they couldn't care less. It's that way with writing. From the first day of school we must leave control of the writing with the child— the choice of topic and the writing itself. Then children write more and care more, even about the appearance of the writing on the page. We teachers must become totally aware of our awful daily temptation to take control away from them, whether by too much prescription or correction or even advice. (Walshe 1981, 5, 8, 9)

Process writing had a huge impact on the teaching of writing on both sides of the Pacific, winning many teacher-devotees who felt liberated from the prescriptive, product-oriented practices of the past. Kamler (1981) made the following observations while researching process-oriented classrooms:

> The extraordinary thing was the process, a process that gave Jill room to pull herself out of a rut; a process that helped her develop an inadequate beginning into a competent end; a process that allowed her to emerge from the completion of one publishing cycle to the next. Egan's classroom allowed Jill to experience her own writing process and develop as a writer . . . her behaviour during the publishing cycle indicated that she had come to value process over product. (88)

The popularity of Process Writing and further developments in psycholinguistics saw the rapid development of a closely linked conceptualization of literacy education: namely, Whole Language. Whole language incorporated Process Writing into its pedagogy and for the next decade was the dominant theory of teaching all aspects of literacy, but especially writing. For many of us this was the "golden age" of writing pedagogy. Unfortunately it didn't last.

In the early '90s a bitter and vociferous opposition to Whole Language emerged. It came from two sources. In the United States it arose from a back-to-basics campaign generated by a narrow, extremist view of science that demanded "evidence-based research" as the basis of any pedagogies associated with the teaching of reading and writing. In Australia it came from educators aligned with poststructural theories, particularly Systemic Functional Linguistics. Both sources claimed (incorrectly) that Whole Language pedagogies precluded the explicit and systematic teaching of "specifics" about language, particularly knowledge about grammar and convention. The rest, as they say, is history.

Since the mid-'90s, a series of heated debates (sometimes referred to as the reading/ writing wars) have continued unabated to the present day. Some have even argued that these debates represent blatant battles for ideological control of policies rather than intellectual attempts to refine theories (Brock 1998; Coles 1998; Green 1996).

However, if there has been a positive outcome to these debates, it is this: *The nexus between new and old theories is crucial for the development of education's knowledge base because it provides a platform for a healthy continuity of development for the profession.* I believe that the spin-off from these heated debates has been considerable. Whole Language pedagogies, together with insights from Systemic Functional Linguistics, provided detailed frameworks for the analysis of language structures. This, in turn, introduced literacy educators to the theoretical concepts inherent in such domains of theoretical concern as Discourse Analysis, Genre Theory, and Critical Literacy—all of which informed the development of a "social view of language." The innovative Four Roles/Sources Model of reading has its roots in the social view of reading (Luke and Freebody 1999). Underpinning all of these concepts is advocacy of using writing to further the social good by addressing issues of equity and social justice. Despite the hostile adversarial stances taken by some who were involved in the reading/writing wars, the subsequent construction of new insightful theories was, in my opinion, a positive outcome.

As mentioned above, the downside of the rapid emergence of all these new, productive theoretical domains is that it creates what Wurman calls "information anxiety" in teachers (Wurman 1989, 2000). This, in turn, leads to what one of my doctoral students, Glenn Short, described as "a condition of theory deficit" in the teaching profession, which sets in train a *"cycle of professional disempowerment."* Short goes on to argue that when this happens teachers "develop survival strategies aimed at creating the illusion of visibility—the illusion that they are meeting the theoretical and policy demands involving the new theories they're hearing about." (Short 2002, 684). The upsurge in sales of student workbooks with ready-to-use lessons and themes that (allegedly) explicitly teach the skills and knowledge in these new theories (with black-line masters) is one indicator of this cycle in action. So, too, is the disengagement of the students who work their way through the worksheets, that (allegedly) provide opportunities for practice and scaffolds that support learning.

In my opinion Lorraine Wilson's book can reverse this cycle of professional disempowerment. She has managed to bring together the new theories that have emerged from Systemic Functional Linguistics, Genre Theory, Discourse Analysis, Critical Literacy, A Social Theory of Language, and Quality Teaching and seamlessly connected them to the theoretical principles in Whole Language and Process Writing.

What I found most compelling in Lorraine's book is her ability to adopt the roles of teacher-educator and K–6 teacher simultaneously. She does it so subtly I almost missed it. For example, in the role of teacher-educator she makes her values and beliefs about the purpose(s) for teaching writing explicit early in the text. We learn that she is passionate about writing being a medium for constructing and changing worldviews, especially with respect to social justice. In the numerous teaching ideas, units of work, activities, and so forth that she describes throughout the book, she never loses sight of, or retreats from, this set of beliefs. It is a superb example of curriculum consistency that integrates values, theory, and practice. Another example is her conviction that if one is going to be a teacher of writing one should also engage in writing—and publish that writing. She does this very subtly by sprinkling her own poems at relevant points throughout the book. The message I took from this practice was, *Here is an educator who practices what she preaches.* It made me resolve to write more and share it with my students. Yet another example of this consistency is the list of eight points (on page 9), which describe in explicit detail what a program of writing based on a worldview of social justice and participatory democracy looks like.

She switches to her K–6 teacher hat when she describes and shares the ideas and concepts she's developed to support teachers. It's obvious she's tried them out in classrooms. It's also obvious that she's reflected on them and modified them in subsequent trials. Classroom teachers will find the Retrieval Charts and Character Construction Charts immediately useful. They will find her ideas on *building on what we already know works* reassuring and innovative. The details of how to use picture books, pop culture, television cartoons, similes and metaphors, and children's magazines to develop and teach units of work that will produce the kinds of writers she values will intrigue and excite them.

She combines both teacher-educator and K–6 classroom teacher hats in the chapter titled Writing as Social Practice. Here she describes lessons in which her students were encouraged to teach *her* to use *their* literacies. The resulting Guides for Learning, which her students constructed, are eloquent testimony to her skill as a classroom practitioner. They cover such things as how to write words using SMS technology, how to win at Pokemon and related computer games, and how to fill out a tennis score sheet.

I recommend this book to all teachers who teach writing. Not only might you have an "Archimedes moment," but the way you teach writing will change forever.

Brian Cambourne
University of Wollongong

Works Cited

Brock, P. 1998. "Breaking Some of the Myths—Again." *The Australian Journal of Language and Literacy* 21 (1): 8–26.

Coles, G. 1998. *Reading Lessons: The Debate over Literacy*. New York: Hill and Wang.

Edelsky, C. 1999. "The Psycholinguistic Guessing Game: A Political-Historical Retrospective." In *Reflections and Connections: Essays in Honor of Kenneth S. Goodman's Influence on Language Education*, edited by A. M. Marek and C. Edelsky, 3–27. Cresskill, NJ: Hampton Press.

Green, B. 1996. "Manners, Morals, Meanings." In *Teaching the English Subjects: Essays on English Curriculum History and Australian Schooling*, edited by B. Green and C. Beavis, 204–30. Geelong, Australia: Deakin University Press.

Kamler, B. 1981. "One Child, One Teacher, One Classroom." In *Donald Graves in Australia: "Children Want to Write . . . ,"* edited by R. D. Walshe, 73–88. Sydney: Primary English Teaching Association.

Luke, A., and P. Freebody. 1999. "A Map of Possible Practices: Further Notes on the Four Resources Model." *Practically Primary: Resources for Reading* 4 (2): 5–9.

Short, G. 2002. *Political Control, Subversion and Survival: A Grounded Theory of the Disempowerment of a Profession.* Unpublished doctoral thesis, Faculty of Education, University of Wollongong, NSW, Australia.

Walshe, R. D. 1981. "Donald Graves in Australia." In *Donald Graves in Australia: "Children Want to Write . . ."* Edited by R. D. Walshe. Sydney: Primary English Teaching Association.

Wurman, R. S. 1989. *Information Anxiety.* New York: Doubleday.

———. 2000. *Information Anxiety 2.* Indianapolis, IN: QUE.

ACKNOWLEDGMENTS

Education is a force for changing the world. School programs can be liberatory and empowering or alienating and confidence sapping. School programs impact who students become and the lives they lead. A school curriculum is grounded in beliefs about learning and in beliefs about life in general, or a worldview. It is only when we have identified a particular worldview or vision for the world's people that we can set about planning a curriculum that will turn this vision into reality.

My thanks to teachers Shirl Ramage, Annie Drennan, Vicky McCormack, Helen Lockart, Jenny Hodges, Leanne Schulz, Jan Hayes, Jenni Smith, Wendy White, Di Woodburn, Mandy Jones, Robin Perkins, and Fiona McKenzie, whose classrooms reflect the values they hold for the world's people. I thank principal Tony Hilton for continuing to make me welcome at Moonee Ponds West Primary School.

I am indebted also to Adele, Aris, Freya, Georgia, Jacqui, Jessica, and Lexie, current and former students of Moonee Ponds West Primary School, who spent time talking with me about their memories of learning to write.

To all those parents who have given permission for their children's work to be included in this publication, thank you.

Lastly, my sincere thanks to acquisitions editor Danny Miller, for his ongoing support and enthusiasm, and to production editor Elizabeth Valway, for her invaluable editorial contribution.

Lorraine Wilson

WRITING TO LIVE

CHAPTER 1

A WORLDVIEW

*Without a perspective on the future, conceivable as a desired future,
there can be no human venture. As an introduction to, preparation
for, and legitimation of particular forms of social life, education
always presupposes a vision of the future.*

—ROGER SIMON (1992, 139–51)

This book is for educators who hope for change in the world; who wish for greater compassion and understanding between the world's peoples; who understand the need for a more equitable distribution of the world's resources; who believe in the need for global agreement on environmental issues; who understand that democracy is more than a political system where the wealthy have unfair influence in the nomination of electoral candidates. How we as teachers envision the world shapes how and what we teach in our classrooms, for our vision shapes our perceptions of our students and the futures we wish for each of them.

Matthew, a fourth grader, was blown away by his meeting with poet Bruce Salau while on a three-day school camping trip at Sunnystones in country Victoria. Note in his writing the quiet confidence he has for his future. Anything he aspires to seems possible. Note too in this, his first draft, that getting his thoughts down is his first priority. His class teacher, Jenny Hodges, has nurtured the children's belief in themselves as learners and writers; in this classroom, concern for correct spelling and form does not prevent the children's using writing exploratively and wonderingly. Of course, attention is paid to the writing conventions at the editing stage.

Sunny Stones Reflections
My favourite thing at the camp was beach volley ball, Bruce's poems, and I think Bruce's poems came to my mind and got to my heart. And I have also made up a little poem myself.

> To Bruce,
> Bruce's Poems.
> Your poems are very good that's what I see
> They are as good as the whistling
> Lullaby right up in the trees
> And as good as the smooth breeze.

Your poems are brighter than the high sky
And brighter than the people's cry.
When you write, poems are what you write
You do them when there's a beautiful sight.

I love your poems Bruce that's why I wrote a poem to you Bruce, because you got me into it. I hope I'll be a poem artist just like you. Your poems also reminded me at camp last year how I saw an echidna on the ground, running to its home like a frightened animal and when the great times happened to me. I am looking forward to writing more storys at any time. in my life and I am looking forward to seeing you again but I wish it is sooner than later. I think you have really good poems and think you are one of the best poets and I think I am going to be one too and I want to be the best. I want to thank you for inspiring me.

—MATTHEW, GRADE 4

Participatory Democracy

Participatory democracy, where people have the right to participate in decisions that affect their lives, means all voices are heard. A system where those with wealth or those with influence or those who belong to certain groups can overrule majority decisions is not a democracy. A system where the mass media is controlled by a powerful few is not democracy (Edelsky 1999).

School literacy programs can educate for democracy or can educate to repress some groups while empowering others. Where schools are tightly controlled from the top, and where what is taught and how it is taught and when it is taught is decided apart from the students themselves, large numbers of those students are doomed to failure and, hence, to leaving school early. The school system itself becomes the agent that denies education to the very children it is funded to teach.

One of the great fault lines running through discussion about education creates two camps that might be labelled "education for democracy" and "education for profits." The former says that schools should be equipping students with skills they'll need to sustain (or possibly to create) a democratic society. The latter, in its purest from, says that school should be preparing students to be productive workers in order to sustain a booming economy. (Kohn 1999, 118)

Valuing Diversity

This book is for those teachers who value all students; who value diversity of skin color, gender, physical and intellectual abilities, social class, religion, nationality, and culture. It is for teachers who are prepared to learn from their students; who see learning as a partnership between child, home, and school; who wish for all children to leave school excited by learning, confident in their potential to contribute to and work toward a more just and equitable society.

This book is for teachers who do not see the world in simple binaries, but who are hopeful of working toward a peaceful, caring world society, where people from different groups and different nations display respect and compassion for one another.

The Binary View

People are
white/black
employed/unemployed
literate/illiterate
educated/uneducated
rich/poor
happy/sad

Wait!
What about the shades in between?
Pink, yellow, brown?

And are
all white people educated
all black people uneducated?
Are all employed people literate
all unemployed people illiterate?
Are all rich people happy
all poor people unhappy?

—Lorraine Wilson

This book is for teachers who feel privileged to be in close company with children entrusted to them by their parents; who delight in seeing their students each morning whether they are rich or poor, monolingual, bilingual, or trilingual; whether they are flying or struggling with learning. How interesting life is in our classrooms because of the diversity of our students. Imagine if all students were the same: if they all spoke the same language, if they all looked the same, if they had all had the same experiences. How predictable each day would be. The aim of school programs should never be to contain difference or produce conformity; it should be to promote understanding of those who are different and to explore ways of living and working together harmoniously.

Stop reading right now if you support mandated state curriculum and testing. Standardized curriculum and testing cannot help but alienate children of poverty, children for whom English is a second or third language, and children of cultural groups other than the mainstream white middle class. State-mandated curriculum and testing is developed outside of schools and dooms all those who are not of the mainstream dominant group to failure. This for me is discrimination. The Declaration of the Rights of the Child by the General Assembly of the United Nations as Unanimously Adopted on November 20, 1959, states: "The child shall be protected from practices that discriminate against people—especially against people's race or religion. The child should be brought up in a spirit of understanding, tolerance, friendship among peoples, peace and universal brotherhood."

While all children are similar in some ways, each child is uniquely different from all other children. Each child is a member of a particular nation, ethnic group, social class, geographic region, community, family group. Each child is physically different, with differing health needs. Each child has different intellectual and emotional needs. Each child possesses a wealth of language and life experiences upon entering school. Each child's life experiences differ.

Bailey James, my grandnephew, has not yet started school. He is a little boy with special needs. In preparation for his first year at school his mom and dad have visited six different primary schools in their search for a school that will value him.

Bailey James

He's six now
and beautiful
with big brown eyes
rosy cheeks
and enthusiastic hugs.

He's six now
in his second year
at kindergarten.
He was not ready
for school.

He's six now
a little different
to other children—
his immaturity
his frustration
his anger.

He's six now.
Next year
he goes to school.
Teacher,
this is our child.
Please care.

—LORRAINE WILSON

For teachers to value all students, they must be quite passionate—about teaching and about all students. They do not feel wronged when working with groups other than mainstream, white, middle-class children; that is, immigrant children, poor children, or children with disabilities. To be fair, teachers, too, need to feel valued; they too need support; they need appropriate resources in working with whichever students they are privileged to teach. They must be free to design learning programs centered in the students themselves; programs that value these learners and that connect and soar with them.

Developing Relevant Learning Programs.

"Culturally relevant pedagogy (Ladson-Billings 1994) means that teaching and curriculum are constructed with, from, and for students" (Meyer 2002, 459). Curriculum relevant to all students is best developed on local school sites. Decisions about what and when to teach cannot be divorced from the students themselves. Doing so assumes that all students are the same. They are not. Students all bring different skills and knowledge with them into their classrooms. Teaching involves finding out about this existing knowledge and building on it in the classroom. Teaching is about making connections with students. Student abilities and interests inform curriculum. Anonymous officials sitting in state offices who do not know the students in individual schools cannot possibly make these connections. Only those who work with students daily, who know their interests, their existing skills and knowledge, and their needs, can plan for their learning.

Holistic educators have always argued that curriculum decisions about what to teach and when to teach it are the right of classroom teachers. They have argued for a language curriculum that develops critically questioning students, and not for one that promotes the passive transmission of knowledge. As Bess Altwerger and Elizabeth Saavedra so aptly stated:

> Whole language educators must once again acknowledge the political role that literacy plays in maintaining systems of power and domination in a class society. With the current return to homogenous tracking, standardised testing, hierarchical basal schemes, and state-approved text book adoption lists, this political role of literacy, which whole language threatened to disrupt, has been firmly reinstated. Those teachers who are struggling to maintain their whole language perspectives must understand that in doing so they are not only defending an instructional model for literacy, but a political stance toward education. Classroom literacy can never be politically neutral. Literacy can be taught either as a tool of political inquiry or of passive transmission. (1999, p xi)

For students to feel valued and see relevance in school for them, they must, in a sense, see themselves in the school curriculum; the history they learn in their classroom must include the histories of their families. Of course by sharing family histories, and hence the histories of different immigrant groups, they come to see there is not just one history for one country. There are many histories.

If all students are to feel valued in school, decisions about what is learned are most appropriately made at school level. Community members and teachers might work together to identify important elements of their school curriculum. Empowering students so they are proud of who they are and believe they have a contribution to make to society on leaving school is dependent on how their school experiences construct them as people. Whether they leave school confident in their abilities to participate in decision making at different levels of government relates to how school programs have valued and nurtured them.

Aspendale Gardens Primary School is situated on the outskirts of Melbourne, a city of nearly 4,000,000 people. The school backs onto the Edithvale wetlands, a treasured natural resource amid the suburban sprawl. The wetlands play a huge role in the children's class work and were the inspiration for this year's school theatrical performance in which every child took part. While some of the older students had individual roles, all children took part representing the different creatures of the wetlands. Kindergarten children were the mini-beasts with different classes being ants, snails, soldier ants, ladybirds, and butterflies. First and second graders were the birds, with the different classes being magpies, pelicans, black swans, blue wrens, and ravens. The performance was a school community event with parents assisting in the making of costumes and backstage management. The play told the story of a bird called Latham's snipe, which migrates without resting or feeding from Japan to Edithvale every year, a distance of 7,000 km.

This is a marvellous example of school and community members working together to construct curriculum that is relevant and important to the lives of the children. Throughout this book I describe classroom language/literacy practice aimed at advancing the learning of each child by beginning with each child's current understandings and building from there.

Language as Representing the World

Writing about language representing our worlds, James Britton said, "that we construct a representation of the world as we experience it, and from this representation, the cumulative record of our own past, we generate expectations concerning the future; expectations which, as moment by moment the future becomes the present, enable us to interpret the present" (1972, 12). As we experience the world we store our representations of it so that when we see the same thing again we have the capacity to remember it. Once we have language, we are able to operate on our representations of the world and, following further experiences, modify and revise them. Language enables us to work on our representations— to wonder, to question, to pose alternate possibilities. That is, we use language to learn.

Bus

Bus stop
A bus ticket
I ride on the bus
We missed the bus
I can go by myself now
Clouds of thick black smoke
Why do the buses pollute the air?
I'll write a letter to the bus company.
I'll agitate for tighter environmental controls.

—LORRAINE WILSON

Language as symbol to construct the world; language to operate on that construction.

Speaking and writing, as expressive modes of language, allow us to construct and order our lives, our experiences, our worlds. Elementary-age children all use language to represent their worlds. They can be challenged to construct the world tomorrow. "Writing the world includes writing a world that is not here yet. For people who participate in a democracy, for people who work with others to create a better future, it is not important only to write the world as it is, it is essential to write the world into being that it is not yet" (Bomer 2004, 7).

Only when we have identified a future can we set some goals toward which to aspire. Grade 5–6 students in Annie Drennan and Shirl Ramage's classroom were asked to write about the futures they hoped for.

> The future that I'm waiting for is be to an inventor or engineer. I would live in a little cottage by the sea. I would work in the city with electrical and solar powered cars. Then the air would be fresher and the grass would be greener. When I go home I would listen to the rain on my tin roof.
>
> —Kelly, grade 5

> In the future I want the world to be a place where I can have kids and not be worried about them every second, a place where there's no poverty and everyone stand on the one level, everyone's equal.
>   I want a world where nobody's ever depressed—or maybe I don't. If I lived in a perfect world life wouldn't have the twists and turns that it does have now. I could never feel the emotions of worried or scared. I don't actually think I want a world like that.
>
> —Paige, grade 5

> My future. It seems so very far away, and yet the future is tomorrow and the next day and the next. I hope I finish high school successfully, and with good results. Then I want to travel the world. I want to visit the countries that got bombed in 2001 and 2002 and see cities rebuilt. I want to be in places of happy faces living in their new houses. I don't want to see people living in the gutter, eating rubbish and begging.
>   I want to be able to go to sleep at night knowing there are no terrorism threats to the world. Why do people have to have the knowledge that a war might erupt or someone might be stabbed and tortured to death? Whenever we turn on the news there are two bad things in the world to one good thing. It should be the other way around.
>   In the future I desperately hope there are cures for deadly diseases like cancer, that rip families apart so easily these days. No-one at all deserves to have their life snatched away from them, no matter what they've done. Everyone makes mistakes.
>
> —Lexie, grade 5

Currently war is consuming much media space. My teacher friends and I have noticed that more fifth- and sixth-grade students are choosing to voluntarily write about war. Rhys wrote about the war in Iraq, where Australian soldiers were deployed alongside U.S. troops. Note how Rhys is challenging that reality. In contrast to the reality of the war in Iraq, Rhys constructs a world for the Iraqi citizens where they "live in peace together."

> I think the war is stupid.
>
> Australian forces shouldn't be over in Iraq. We are doing the American's dirty work for them. Lots of men are losing their lives because of America. If they want to go to war, I say let them but we should take no part in it.
>
> If I had my way, our soldiers would be here where they belong and it's like Bush is sending them to their graves. Why should the soldiers lose their lives just because of someone who wants them to defend him. I don't think it's fair that the soldiers don't get to have a say in this. I feel that if the soldiers don't want to go to war then they shouldn't have to. They should be able to be in charge of their lives, not George Bush. He is treating them like a baby; he's making decisions for them.
>
> I feel sorry for the Iraqis—the civilians are getting killed every day because of two people—George Bush and Saddam Hussein. I think George Bush is heartless getting his men to slaughter children and their families. What did they do to him? Nothing—he should let them start a new life and put their troubles aside and start afresh and live in peace together.
>
> —RHYS, GRADE 6

Valuing All Art Forms

As important as verbal language is in representing and making sense of the world, there are other expressive art forms mankind has used through the ages for this same purpose. These include drama, dance, music, and the visual arts. All of these art forms should be part of each school curriculum. The more ways we have of representing and reading the world, the richer we are; each art form allows different shades of meaning, different ways of knowing. To be fully literate in our world is to be able to read all mankind's symbol systems. . . . the art galleries, the theatres, the libraries. In classrooms children talk and write and act out and paint scientific and social cultural understandings, all as part of a meaning-making process. Individual children should sometimes have preferences about the media they use to express themselves on particular issues. Not all of us are equally confident and competent in any one art medium. Think of how works by famous choreographers, composers, sculptors, and painters have enriched our lives. These gifted creators often say what they mean, in one particular art medium. Similarly, some students can better express their thoughts by sketching or dancing than by speaking or writing. Sometimes the act of allowing students to choose their preferred medium first to clarify some issue enhances how and what they later say or write.

Summary: A Worldview and Teaching Writing

Teaching programs are not neutral: they construct reality in particular ways. Some programs value certain cultures more than others, some languages over others, some literary texts over others. Teachers must be aware of the link between teaching programs and particular constructions of the world.

How can any one of us plan a writing program for children if we do not first consider the bigger picture? What type of world do we wish for these students? What type of people do we hope they will become? How will the class approach to writing contribute to these ideals? What chance of success does each student have with this program?

In this book, I aim to link the writing program with a worldview of social justice and participatory democracy. Such a program

- develops student writers by valuing who they are, by valuing their families, their languages, and their literacies.
- helps each student find his voice through writing and giving him the freedom to write about things important to him.
- is about children writing for different purposes, all important to the lives they are living now and wish to live in the future. It allows children to write exploratively and wonderingly.
- is inclusive, starts with each child's existing understandings about language and about writing, and aims to make him confident as a language user so he is able to use his writing to interact with the world around him.
- develops values of respect and compassion by living these values in the classroom.
- includes the study of concepts basic to a study of social justice.
- is about writing critically, being aware of how language is used to construct and represent events and groups of people. It is about teaching children the relationship between language and power and how to be able and willing to read and write critically, so that they can act upon their worlds and work for change.
- is developed on-site by teachers. What is taught and how it is taught is seen as the professional responsibility of the teachers who work with particular students.

References

Altwerger, B., and E. R. Saavedra. 1999. Foreword to *Making Justice Our Project*. Urbana, IL: National Council of Teachers of English.

Bomer, R. 2004. "Dimensions of Writing to World: Looking at Critical Composing from Three Directions." *Talking Points*. www.ncte.org/pubs/journals/tp/contents/111833.htm.

Britton, J. 1972. *Language and Learning*. Great Britain: Pelican Books.

Declaration of the Rights of the Child, General Assembly of the United Nations. 1959.

Edelsky, C., ed. 1999. "On Critical Whole Language: Why, What, and a Bit of How." In *Making Justice Our Project*. Urbana, IL: NCTE.

Kohn, A. 1999. *The Schools Our Children Deserve*. New York: Houghton Mifflin.

Ladson-Billings, G. 1994. *The Dreamkeepers: Successful Teachers of African American Children*. San Francisco: Jossey-Bass.

Meyer, R. 2002. "Captives of the Script: Killing Us Softly with Phonics." *Language Arts*, 79, no. 6 (July).

Simon, R. 1992. "Empowerment as a Pedagogy of Possibility. " In *Becoming Political: Readings and Writings in the Politics of Literacy Education*, edited by P. Shannon, 139–51. Portsmouth, NH: Heinemann.

CHAPTER 2

Writing Critically

Critical literacy . . . moves beyond a description
of society and into an interrogation of it.

—Linda Christensen (1999, 212)

Critical Literacy

The last decade has seen "critical literacy" be the hot topic in the language education community. Basic tenets of critical literacy are that texts are not neutral: writers have values and the texts they create are value laden. Through texts, social identities and power relations are established (Luke, O'Brien, and Comber 2001). The challenge for readers is to identify the decisions made by creators in their texts, which construct people and events in particular ways, and then to decide whether this is how they, the readers, wish to be positioned. The challenge for writers is twofold: how to write to challenge particular representations and stereotypes, and how to compose texts that represent people and events with fairness and justice.

Arguments for the need for critical literacy center around the control of the mass media by fewer and fewer individuals who, of necessity, are among the world's richest people and, hence, have a large influence on elected governments. "For many years western media and news agencies have dominated the international flow of news. Third World spokespersons have long protested the biased portrayals of their countries in western news and called for a two-way and balanced news flow. A more basic Third World concern is the threat to cultural integrity and sovereignty from the flood of western advertising messages and other cultural products, as well as news" (Herman 1992, 16).

Critical literacy is also imperative in this age because of the opportunity provided via the worldwide Web to any individual, to distribute any information, on any topic, right around the world in just a few seconds. Web viewers must have strategies that allow them to deconstruct Web texts to see how groups and events are being constructed before determining if they, as readers, are happy to accept such views. Ordinary people need to understand the power of language in making the world the way it is. "Whole language educators . . . view language as a cultural resource, and believe that access to power and equity in our culture is contingent upon control of many forms of language.

They therefore aim to create classrooms which support learners in the acquisition of the skills and knowledge necessary for understanding the links between language and status and language and power" (Wilson 1997, 118).

Basic to an understanding of critical literacy is knowing that no text is value free. Critical literacy enables readers to study texts and to identify how language and visuals have been used to construct particular representations of people and events, and to identify the values of the creators. War texts, for example, need to be read critically. During the recent war on Iraq the term *surgical hit* was frequently used to describe bombing attacks. The medical metaphor softened the impact of military attacks that resulted in the deaths of innocent civilians.

Dr. Annabelle Lukin reports how President Bush described the first night of the bombing of Afghanistan in October 2001, in which, according to media reports, at least twenty Afghanis were killed, in the following way:

> "These carefully targeted actions are designed to disrupt the use of Afghanistan as a terrorist base of operations and attack the military capability of the Taliban regime." The quote from Bush can be contrasted with the famous speech of Churchill's, in which he said "We will fight them on the beaches." While Churchill represented those events as humans acting on humans, Bush, together with his team of speech writers, has in this case construed the events as abstract entities acting on abstract entities.
>
> For instance, the only agent in this example from Bush is "These carefully targeted actions." This agent is not human, it is not even a physical, tangible object, like a bomb. It is a grammatical entity created by turning the verb "act" into the noun "action." (2003)

Reading Curriculum Documents Critically

If no text is value free, then all curriculum documents are value laden. As teachers, we must read critically all curriculum documents, particularly those which are state mandated, and ask ourselves

What are the values of the creators of these documents?

Upon which theory of learning are these documents based?

What type of future is envisioned for each student with this curriculum?

Does this curriculum disadvantage any group of students?

Which students are advantaged by this curriculum?

What is the real purpose of this curriculum?

Critical Literacy Understandings

In my own teaching of critical literacy, I aim to have children come to the following understandings: Critical literacy involves knowing

- All writing is a human construct.
- Writers have values.
- Writing involves writers making decisions.
- Writers' values impact the decisions they make.
- Although readers make their own meanings, writers aim to shape reader meanings.
- Not all groups in our society have equal power.
- Not all groups in our society have equal opportunity to express their views through written texts; some voices are silent.
- Readers can reject particular stereotypes and points of view. (Wilson 2002, 127–28)

While the term *critical literacy* includes both reading and writing, I think it is true to say that most of the work done so far in schools has focused on reading critically. Much good work has involved students analyzing or deconstructing texts to identify the strategies used by creators to manipulate reader's interpretations.

Reading Practices and Critical Literacy

Reading critically or reading as a text analyst involves one of several different reading practices. Luke and Freebody (1999) identified the following reading practices in their Four Resources Model: code breaker, text participant, text user, and text analyst. *Code breaking* is using a range of strategies to enter and get inside a text. *Text participating* is reading to make meaning. *Text using* is using the text to satisfy some life interest or need. *Text analyzing* is the critical literacy-reading practice. Luke and Freebody argue that to read for today's society one must be competent in all four of these reading practices. Importantly, you cannot read a text critically unless you have participated in the text. That is, you must construct meaning before you can analyze for a critical perspective. "With regard to the critical dimension, it is important that social and educational practices need to be 'meaningful' before they can become 'critical,' or be made so" (Durrant and Green 2000, 104–105).

Critical literacy is much more than reading to understand: it requires the reader to stand back from the text and to interrogate it with questions like the following:

What authority has this writer to say this?

What do other authorities on this topic have to say?

What information of relevance has been left out?

Who is excluded from this text?

How has this writer used language or visuals to shape the group or event being described in a particular way?

What have the creators of this text got to gain from constructing this group/event in this way?

Is this construction one I accept?

How might I respond to this construction?

The last question is important. For if we aim to develop critically literate students for the purpose of working toward a more socially just world, it will not be sufficient that students are able to deconstruct texts. They must know ways of taking action. They might write to creators, to support or to berate, on the basis of their analysis. They might construct an alternate text. They might start a petition gaining the support of others regarding a particular representation within the text. Being critically literate means knowing not only how to interrogate texts and how to identify those strategies used to position readers, but also how to use dissenting voices. Being critically literate is not a passive condition; it involves taking action.

As mentioned above, to read critically is to read differently. It is more than reading for understanding. To read critically is to be able to identify the quite deliberate choice and use of language to construct reality in particular ways. It is to identify those events and people who are foregrounded in texts and those who are left out. Critical literacy is not something taught after children read as text participants and are text users. Critical literacy is not just for advanced readers. Critical literacy is for all students of all ages throughout the primary school.

Texts used for critical reading in classrooms extend beyond print texts. They include those texts the students read and view out of school hours, texts such as TV cartoons and programs, computer games, newspaper sports columns and comic strips, and the many popular-culture magazines devoured by students of all ages. (See the examples later in this chapter.)

My hope is that working with students in reading print texts critically will extend to their reading everyday life situations and asking, "Why?" That is, that critical literacy becomes critical living; for example, in reading the seating arrangements of a large commercial airliner, you might ask, Who is seated in the plush seats at the front of the plane? Who is seated in cramped conditions at the back? Could there be an alternate seating arrangement? Perhaps the old and frail could be seated in the first-class seats. Perhaps all seats could be the same size.

Critical Writing

But we need also to address with students the issue of critical writing; how the language and visuals they choose to use construct events and peoples. Of course critical writing includes students writing critically about a text read, but it must also mean that students write with consideration for how they, too, are representing particular social groups. They need to address the following types of questions as they construct their fictional texts:

Which gender will I make the main character?

Which racial origin and culture will the main character be?

Which age and in what physical condition will the main character be?

Are my characters falling into mainstream stereotypes?

How well does this character of mine represent other members of this group (the aged; the blind)?

Am I implying all members of this group are like my portrayal of this one member?

Who am I excluding from this text?

When constructing a factual text they must ask,

Is this true?

Am I writing fact or opinion?

What is the supporting evidence for what I am writing?

Who are the different groups (individuals) involved in this event?

Have I generalized about a group from the actions of one member?

Have I ignored the perspective of one of the groups involved?

Have I accurately represented the different perspectives?

What do other writers say on this subject?

Have I used language factually and precisely?

Have I used language emotively?

What do I have to gain from writing as I have?

Critical writing has the potential to create new ways of being, as when writers consciously create different life paths and different life roles for particular social groups— rich/poor, old/young, white/colored. Of course, children's capacity to write with consciousness of the ways they portray people and events in their writing will be sharpened by their participation in classroom critical discussion and by analyzing the texts of others.

Developing Awareness of Concepts Basic to an Understanding of Social Justice

Parallel with learning to read and write critically, children must have the opportunity to develop concepts basic to understanding what is meant by "a socially just society." Children cannot detect elitism in texts if they do not know about wealth and poverty. Concepts necessary for understanding social justice include

gender, physical impairment, race, culture, social class, religion,

poverty, employment, unemployment, homelessness, social services, power, bullying, war, peace, racism, sexism, ageism, discrimination, persecution, indigenous peoples, colonisation, invasion, migration, settlement, refugees, justice, fairness, injustice, crime, punishment, democracy, government, environment, sustainability, industry, pollution, natural resources, industrial waste

Family Together

As wind ripples the water
in the grey evening light
a family sits together on the jetty
fishing.
The sudden movement of the rod
signals a catch.
The line pulls taut and
the fish flees frantically
under the jetty
seeking freedom.
But the catch is landed
and lies gasping
on the hard wooden boards.

Excitement lights the young child's face
and he watches
as the fish is measured.

Grandparents, parents and children, enjoy as one.
No age discrimination here.

—Lorraine Wilson

In areas where there is a mix of social groups, teaching to understand cultural differences is more immediate and more real—and more possible. Still, it is crucial that all students develop social justice understandings. Children who attend schools with largely homogenous student populations are in danger of having a very sheltered, limited view of the world. Students who live in affluent areas, sleep in their own bedrooms, have their own computers, are driven to school in expensive motor vehicles, and are members of the mainstream cultural group will have a very narrow vision of the world unless schools and families make a concerted effort to remove them from their comfort zone and introduce them to the world outside and to other cultural and economic groups. Schools with different pupil populations in the same vicinity might set out to jointly develop a local park, plan some environmental project, or stage a musical performance together. Only by being together and working toward a common goal can we, the world's people, get to know one another.

Classroom Practice

Responding Critically to the Texts of Others

The challenge for teachers has been to find strategies that enable primary-school-aged children to use language to exercise power and to question practices of privilege and injustice. What, exactly, does the teacher ask of children to help them identify the decisions made by creators of texts, decisions that shape the representation of particular social groups? Which strategies will enable children to stand back from text and identify the way the writers and illustrators construct characters and manipulate how readers understand the text? Which classroom practices enable children to write with awareness of their own portrayal of varying social groups?

Identifying Author Decisions and Author Messages

Simple picture storybooks can carry powerful author messages about society. Such a book is *In Flanders Fields* by Norman Jorgensen and Brian Harrison-Lever, set in the First World War. As the story begins, it is Christmas morning and hostilities have ceased temporarily. A young Allied soldier sees a robin trapped in barbed wire in the center of no-man's-land. The young soldier makes his way out to rescue the bird and set it free. Enemy rifles are trained on him.

Session 1 The book is read aloud, up to the point where the young Allied soldier walks out onto no-man's-land to rescue the trapped robin. The artwork shows an enemy soldier aiming his rifle at the Allied soldier. The children write what they think will happen to the Allied soldier.

The teacher finishes reading the story. Children comment as they wish.

The children move back and sit in a whole-class circle. In turn each child reads his prediction of what might happen to the soldier. As the predictions are read, each writer places his prediction with other like predictions in the middle of the circle. The children's predictions are entered on a chart. One grade 1–2 came up with the following predictions:

> He puts the other soldiers in jail. (1 child)
>
> He saves the bird, but there is some fighting in the process. (3)
>
> He saves the bird and is not hurt. (6)
>
> He rescues the bird and leaves the army. He does not fight anymore. (3)
>
> The soldier dies. (8)

This activity helps children see that authors exercise choice as they write and that what they believe and value influences the choices they make.

Session 2 The teacher reads the book aloud a second time. The class refers to the predictions made in the first session and reviews them from the chart.

The teacher asks the children to think about the author's decision at the point in the story where the soldier was not fired upon. The children are asked to think quietly about the story and how the author finished it—soldiers from both sides are heard singing "Silent Night," some in German, some in English. Discussion does not occur here because the aim is for each child to think about the author's message in this book and not to be unduly influenced by those children with strong opinions.

The children then write what they think the author's message is.

The MASeG Is DON'T HOT ATHA PePoL
(The message is saying "Don't hurt other people.")

—Luke, grade 1

He wants us to Remember the PePole who freed our country And its Not Good To fight.

—Robbie, grade 2

Because Hes saying the wold shol Be ONE!
(Because he's saying the world should be ONE!)

—Bianca, grade 3

This book is about trusting one enother. If you show peace you will always get something good out of it or get something back and if you do good to others and help others, something good will happen to you. Showing peace is a good thing.

—Lara, grade 4

Retrieval Charts and the Construction of Gender in Television Cartoons

Jenni Smith and Wendy White invited me to work in their grades 2–3–4 classroom, where the integrated study of the time was Cartoons. They requested that I develop a critical literacy component to the integrated study. To this end I taped at my home some of the cartoons shown on television in the after-school hours. After viewing them, I chose to use several from the *Little Grey Rabbit* series. My critical focus with this particular series was the construction of gender.

- We viewed each of the particular cartoons in the classroom at least three times; the first viewing was purely for enjoyment and meaning making.
- On the second viewing, children worked in pairs watching for information, which they recorded on retrieval charts balanced on their knees as they sat on the carpet. On these charts (see Table 1), which were 16″ × 12″ to give these younger children ample room to make their entries, all the animals in the episode were listed in the left-hand column under the heading Characters. Several key story events in which the different animals were involved were listed in another vertical column. There were spaces left in this column for the children to enter additional story events. The column Describe Characters' Actions/Feelings referred to the particular event in the adjacent column. After this second viewing, the children shared briefly the types of information they were entering.
- A third viewing enabled the children to complete the retrieval of information for each column. The sample in Table 1 was completed by Hanna and Lilliana for the first episode viewed. We noticed that with each sub-

sequent episode, the children included more information on their charts
and the information included was more precise.

The children, who used retrieval charts to extract information from two further episodes
from the same series, were challenged to describe the construction of gender in the series
with the following prompt: Using your retrieval charts, compare what the male characters
do and how they behave, with what the female characters do and how they behave.
Following are some of their responses.

> Females tend to do more work and don't be silly and act like they don't have as much
> energy as the males. They are also quieter and timid.
>   Males have more energy and are usually a bit siller than females. They are shown
> braver and bolder. They don't do as much work either. The girls thought that they
> had to be perfect and posh, like if hare was a girl then they would not have made
> him run beside the boat, the other man would have had to.
>
> —Ali and Holly

> Males had more events than females
> Males were more advenchrues than the females
> Males got the bigger part
> Females are more used as maids
> Males were always more outdoors
> Males were cheeky
> Weman were always more machure (mature)
> Males use more interesting langauge
>
> —Carly and Caitlin

> Females were always dressed in a dress or something like a hood. The cartoonists
> made the females very genouris and some of the males rude, demanding and greedy
> and others were brave heroic and kind. Gentlemen didn't wear a full outfit. Females
> were like servants for the men in a way but they did care for them.
>
> —Emma and Ali

The homeroom teachers and I were pleased with the ability of the children across the class
to use their retrieval charts to draw conclusions about the behavior of each gender in the
cartoon, and to make comparisons. Some of the children indicated in their writing their
perception that it was the creators choosing to make the males and females act in particular ways. For example,

> The cartoonists made the females very genouris and some of the males rude, de-
> manding and greedy and others were brave heroic and kind
>
> —Emma and Ali

These girls are aware that texts are not neutral; rather, they reflect author values.
    In a following session the children were again asked to write, but this time it was
for the purpose of reflecting on, and questioning more generally, gender roles in today's

Table 1 *Tales of Little Grey Rabbit.* **Episode: "Hare and the Easter Eggs"**

Characters	Male/ Female	Clothes	Props/ Things	Events	Describe Characters' Actions/ Feelings
Squirrel	F	Spotted dress Apron	Ribbon Candle Nitting needles	1. HARE DOESN'T COME HOME ONE NIGHT	Fine and comferdable
Grey Rabbit	F	Pale blue dress Aprin	Toy chicken Easter cake	1. HARE DOESN'T COME HOME ONE NIGHT 2. PLANS AN EASTER PARTY FOR EVERYONE	Worried and scared Proud, excited
Hedgehog	M	Tie red shoes Blue dress (this was actually an artist's smock)	Bag bucket	Easter Party	Happy Glad to be there
Wise Owl	M	Feathers	Easter eggs	Easter party	Sneaky suspishes
Speckledy Hen	F	Green bonet Green aprin	Hen eggs	Easter party	excited
Mole	M	Brown vest Purple scarf	Money Shovel Paint eggs	1. TRADES MONEY FOR EGGS	Graetful to lend money
Cat	F	Fur	Milk meat	Listening to Hare's storey	Interested Calm happy
Fox	M	Jacket Vest Shirt			

continues

Table 1   *(Continued)*

Characters	Male/ Female	Clothes	Props/ Things	Events	Describe Characters' Actions/ Feelings
Hare	M	Blue blaser Tie Shirt vest	Branch to bow with (meaning used like a staff)	1. STEALS ONE EGG 2. GOES OUT BY MOONLIGHT FOR MORE EASTER EGGS 3. GIVES CHOCOLATE EGGS TO ALL THE ANIMALS	Cheaky, brave and suspishes 2. confedent sneaky 3. proud hapy
Customer, Mrs. Snowball	F	High heels dress	money		
Shopkeeper, Mrs. Bunting	F	High heels Dress aprin	Easter eggs	1. THINKS SHE HEARS A MOUSE	Angree Suprized shocked

society. They were asked to recall how men and women were constructed in *The Little Grey Rabbit* cartoon series. The writing prompt then was: Is this how life has to be for men and women?

> NO! Life dose not have to be like this Wemon can take risks and men can stay in doors and knit/sew. Girls can run and be brave.
> Girls can be stronger than boys and play outdoors.
>
> —Ali

> I think that the answer is "no" because women have the right to take risks, demand people do something, be heroic, make decisions for themselves and they can still be gentle, kind, trustworthy, mutre (mature) and heaps more plus men have a right to be different or the same because Male and female have a right to be who they are and stay like that forever.
>
> —Emma

In this classroom sequence of lessons the retrieval charts proved a very good vehicle for having students pull data from texts for the purpose of analyzing how the creators were constructing gender roles. The children's written responses show how relatively young children are able to write critically about texts written by others.

Retrieval Charts and the Construction
of Boys in Picture Storybooks

The following work was completed in two grade 5 and two grade 6 classrooms in an outer suburban school. In these classrooms retrieval charts were used to extract data relating to the construction of boys in picture storybooks (Table 2). The first book analyzed was *Tracks* by Gary Crew and Gregory Rogers. This picture storybook tells of a small boy camping out, first in a forest and then in his backyard. It is nighttime. He is out hunting, alone, finding all sorts of animal tracks with the light of a flashlight.

For this retrieval chart, one column, Words/Phrases, required the children to enter words or phrases that they felt had been chosen to shape the character in a particular way. An example of language we discussed as a class is the use of the word *sneaks* in the following line from *Tracks*: "He sneaks under bushes." We listed alternate words the author might have used here: tiptoes, creeps, pushes, crawls, slips. Why, then, *sneaks*? Was it perhaps that *sneaks* has connotations of daring and risk taking?

Session 1　*Tracks* was read aloud to the children, who then individually made entries on their retrieval charts. The book was read aloud a second time while the children added any missing information. Next the children were asked to write in response to the following prompt: Would it have mattered if the main character in *Tracks* had been a girl?

Session 2　The second book analyzed, *The Water Tower* by Gary Crew and Steven Woolman, is a mysterious tale of what happens one hot, dusty afternoon when two boys climb up to the top of a small town's water tower to have a swim. Again, the text was read aloud to all students, who then entered data on the retrieval chart.

After extracting data relating to the construction of boys in both of these Gary Crew books, the children next wrote in response to the prompt, Which boys have been excluded from these texts? In their lists, children included boys who were shy, fat, wore glasses, had dark skin, were in wheelchairs, liked to read, weren't adventurous.

In following sessions the children worked in pairs, using retrieval charts to deconstruct the boy characters in other picture storybooks that were part of a bulk loan from the school library. All books chosen had human characters, not animals dressed as males or females. Each pair of children retrieved information from five to six titles. As work progressed it became evident that not all the children understood what was meant by the Race/Culture heading. Some thought this related just to nationality. Another area of confusion involved identifying particular words or phrases chosen by authors in shaping characters and social groups. The children were unaware that synonyms do not mean exactly the same thing but rather introduce differing shades of meaning.

When all the children had retrieved data from five to six picture storybooks they were asked to review their data and to consider how boys were constructed in these

Table 2   Retrieval Chart

Title Author Illustrator	Main Character Culture/ Race	Age Physical Description	Interests/ Things Done by Character	Clothes Worn	Characteristics	Words/Phrases	Settings	Colors
Tracks Gary Crew and Gregory Rogers								
The Water Tower, Gary Crew and Steven Woolman								

texts: If all we knew about boys came from our reading of these books, we would think boys were . . .

> They would be active, ruff, boystress, they would like to be outside rather than inside. They wear casual clothes so they can move. Sometimes the boys in the picture story book dress up as people like soldiers and pretend to be famous baseball star or something. They are into sport, playing games, having fun. They wouldn't be into sitting around talking to people or reading. They might be into TV. But they are probably more active they would probably watch sport on TV and things like that.
>
> —SAMANTHA

> I think boys are very curious, adventurous, troublesome and immature according to the books we have read. They also like mucking around doing the wrong things, playing with things they are not meant to do and running down the street naked. They are also very interested in everything around them.
>
> —JENNA

Writing Picture Storybooks and Character Construction Charts

Following the work with retrieval charts to deconstruct boy characters in picture storybooks, the children were challenged to construct a boy main character for a picture storybook of their own. This boy character was not to fit the stereotype identified in the previous sessions. I changed the heading on the charts the children had been using to now read Character Construction Charts, and the children spent time thoughtfully trying to create a boy main character unlike those in the many books we had read (Table 3). Watching the children work, it soon became clear that there were different ways of doing this. Some children opted for a character from the excluded group identified earlier (dark-skinned, Asian, with glasses, in a wheelchair, timid, etc.). Others chose the usual healthy Anglo boy but made him interested in matters other than sports and the outdoors; he was more passive than the usual gutsy risk taker. A minority of children constructed a character from the excluded group and made this boy a quieter, more reflective child. Here the students were applying their understandings, gleaned from the deconstruction of books read, to writing critically.

Once each of these student writers had constructed a character, the next job was to write this character into a text for a picture storybook, which they went on to publish. Using retrieval charts to analyze the gender construction of characters in TV cartoons and picture storybooks proved successful. The format gave the children easy access to data, from which they could draw conclusions about the representation of gender in these texts. The various columns clearly showed the different categories of decisions made by creators. Such charts could also be used to study the construction of other groups in texts, for example, the disabled, the elderly, people of different ethnic groups, and the poor.

Using Popular-Culture Magazines for Critical Literacy

Most older elementary-aged children are devout readers of popular-culture magazines. Part of developing literacy programs relevant to children's lives is to bring their texts

Table 3   Character Construction Chart (Clementine)

Title	Main Character Name Age Physical Description	Culture/ Race	Interests/ Things Done by Character	Clothes Worn	Characteristics	Settings	Words/Phrases
	John 9 brown hair brown eyes tanned skin disabled in a wheel chair	Australian	Loves books Stays in his room	Smart clothes	Very shy Likes to be alone happy	His room School Car	Mutters a lot of his words What? bash crash hesitates

into the classroom. At one outer suburban school, grade 5–6 children voted that the text we would use for critical literacy would be *TV Hits*.

Session 1: Who Has Been Excluded?   In the first session my aims were to develop children's understandings that

> texts are not neutral;
>
> texts construct people in particular ways;
>
> some people are excluded from texts.

All children were given a photocopy of an advertisement from *TV Hits*. The page was headed with the following caption: "Style Hot for Him: Sharpen your cool with this month's must-have rockin' essentials." Underneath were photos of fashion items for youths, with prices.

> Rip Curl on Strike shirt—$69.95
>
> Fudge men's black boxer shorts—$27.95
>
> Esprit men's faded jeans—$99.95
>
> Puma Pa La La silver shoes—$240.00
>
> Boile Turbulence sunnies—$249.95
>
> Hot Tuna racing T-shirt—$55.00
>
> The Body Shop of a man Aftershave Balm—$34.00
>
> The Body Shop of a man Antiperspirant/Deodorant—$16.85

The jeans, shirt, boxers and T-shirt photographed were obviously for slim young guys. The children were asked to describe a cool young man according to this advertisement.

> brand names important
>
> has lots of money
>
> is of slim build
>
> wears Western-style fashion
>
> has casual lifestyle
>
> smells nice

Next the children were asked to identify those young men who could not be "cool" according to this ad.

> impoverished
>
> overweight
>
> wears clothes of some other culture

Session 2: How Have the Young Women Been Constructed? How Has Language Been Used to Do This?   The aims were the same as for session 1 but I added: Writers use language to construct people in particular ways.

The children were given a black-and-white photocopy of a full-page article from *TV Hits*. Several copies of the magazine with color photographs were available for the children to see. The page was headed "Star Trends: Low Riders—What Stars Are Wearing." On the page were five color photographs of young female stars wearing low-riding jeans or trousers. In my opinion all were attractively dressed and none were cheaply or scantily clad, but I felt that the accompanying text set out to portray each of the young women as a cheap flesh object. The children responded as follows to these prompts:

1. List all the body parts mentioned in the captions.
   crotch
   bellybutton
   butt
   hip-huggers
   hip
   flesh
   butt-huggin

2. List body parts not mentioned, which might have been.
   waist
   knees
   leg
   brain

3. List the similes and metaphors used.
   a purr-fect fit for pussycats
   may sing like a bird, but she looks like a fox
   Why have these associations been made? Using metaphor and simile, the creator is constructing the young women as soft, cuddly (cats), sweet (singing like a bird), yet also with some cunning (fox).

4. From the text, list all the implied actions (verb phrases) for the female stars. (Some of this we did as a class.)
   are going to take a mile
   are getting down and almost dirty
   had their low-cut jeans specially made
   had to cut the waistbands off their undies
   couldn't bend over without showing just a bit too much butt
   may sing like a bird
   looks like a fox
   know the value of staying hip to trends
   out of spare flesh

Having the students analyze the language in this way helped them identify the construction of these young females as cunning, wily, and prepared to sell flesh to stay on top. An interesting activity would first have been to give the students the photographs without captions and challenge them to write captions and then discuss any differences in their portrayals of the young stars.

Session 3: The Use of Metaphor and Simile to Construct Groups   By way of contrast to the text used above, an article from the same magazine, about the group Destiny's Child, was shown. This page featured one large photograph of the three female members of the group, dressed in quite stunning performance gear, which, in fact, showed as much bare skin (if not more) than the photographs of the page described above. The heading read "Destiny's Child may be the world's No. 1 girl group, but they've slugged their guts out for 11 years to make it happen. *TV Hits* goes inside DC's boot camp for the full story . . ."

The students discussed "boot camp." They knew it was a pretty tough camp attended by military personnel. We then discussed the author's use of it in this text: "*TV Hits* goes inside DC's boot camp." Had the entertainers been in a military boot camp? No. The children came to explain the use of this metaphor by saying the singers had had to work really hard to get to the top. I listed some of the questions asked in this interview:

> You've worked incredibly hard ever since forming the band Girls Tyme in 1990. Has it felt like being in boot camp?
>
> What were the biggest sacrifices you made?
>
> Coming from Texas—hardly the home of R&B—was it hard to break into the industry?

The children were asked to talk with a partner about what the interviewer was doing by asking these questions. The idea of begging a question was introduced.

These two articles, from one magazine with two different feature writers writing about young female stars, exemplified how writers use language to represent their subjects in predetermined ways. In particular, the link was made with the image presented of the two different groups with the two sets of metaphors and similes—boot camp versus purrfect fit, sing like a bird, look like a fox.

Session 4: Writing to Construct One Individual in Different Ways   For the final lesson in this series on pop-culture magazines the children were all given copies of a full-page photo of the pop group *NSYNC and an accompanying article. They were given time to read the article and then were challenged to write two captions to go with the accompanying photograph of each group member. The first set of captions was to construct each of the group members as a clean-living, conservative guy; someone a girl's family would be pleased to see her dating. The second set of captions was to construct each young man as a party animal; someone who lived life on the wild side. I demonstrated how I might do this in writing about band member JC: "JC pays careful attention to detail, color-coordinating jacket and shoes," and "Ideal for a wild night on the town is JC's outfit, featuring loosened tie and untucked shirt."

As I wrote I thought aloud, that, while I could construct JC differently through a different choice of words, I could not lie. There is a difference between saying, "JC has a wild night on the town" and "Ideal for a wild night on the town is JC's outfit." The children found this quite difficult, but if children are to understand critical literacy and the power of language to represent social groups, I feel it is imperative they engage with such writing.

Identifying Design Decisions in the Construction of Gender in Children's Magazines

Upon questioning the lady at my local newsstand recently, I learned of two magazines published especially for nine- to twelve-year-old children. The magazines, *Total Girl* and *K-Zone*, come in sealed clear plastic bags that contain some freebies. The *Total Girl* freebies were a plastic cell phone that contained lip gloss and, in the next month's edition, pink plastic bracelets. In the *K-Zone* magazine the freebies were many: in one edition there were a packet of red licorice candy, a packet of chocolate Nerds, a bookmark promoting the latest edition of Australian stamps, and a miniature book containing the first chapter of *The Slippery Slope*, a newly released novel by Lemony Snicket. Both magazines are published by the same publisher.

The lady at the newsstand handed me *Total Girl* saying, "That's the girls' magazine." She then handed me *K-Zone* saying, "And this is the boys." Curiously, although both magazines are the same shape and overall size, *K-Zone* has sixteen more pages in each edition but costs thirty cents less and, as I said previously, is packaged with more freebies than *Total Girl*. So fellow teacher Fiona McKenzie and I decided to do some comparisons and a critical analysis of these two magazines with her grade 5–6 students. Again, the main focus was gender construction. When Fiona purchased copies at her local newsstand, the news agent also referred to *K-Zone* as "the boys' magazine."

In preparation for the analysis of these texts we copied the contents pages, and also made copies of many of the articles. There were also four copies of the magazines for the children to browse at any time. This was important because we wanted to study the use of color in constructing the readers of each magazine.

Session 1   When the magazines were displayed for the children to see, there was an instant buzz of recognition. A show of hands confirmed that most of the children were familiar with them.

Fiona scattered photocopies of a range of pages from each magazine in the middle of the class circle. Individual children were asked to select a page and identify the magazine from which the page was copied. Every child made a correct identification. Some of the reasons given by the children in their identification were:

It's a diary. Girls keep diaries. (*Total Girl*)

There's flowers around the edges. (*Total Girl*)

It tells facts. (*K-Zone*)

There are cartoon figures. (*K-Zone*)

The children worked in groups of four. Each group had copies of the tables of content, together with copies of articles and pages from each magazine. The instructions for each group were:

1. Read the pages aloud in turn. After reading the contents pages from both magazines, vote on which magazine you would prefer to read. Record each group member's choice and reasons.

2. Compare the two magazines and discuss the differences.

3. Who is represented? Who is not represented?

4. How does the publisher construct boys and girls through these magazines? (What messages do the magazines give/what perceptions are encouraged?)

5. Why does the publisher work to create these perceptions? How might the publisher benefit?

6. What would your group like to tell the publishers of these magazines? (See Figure 2–1.)

It was in the comparison and discussion of the differences between the two magazines that the children were identifying deliberate decisions made by the creators to portray boys and girls in stereotypical ways. Some of the decisions they listed include

Use of color

K-Zone—dark colors; shaded colors;

Total Girl—colorful; light colors; nice soft colors; pink, purple, light blue.

Content

K-Zone—jokes; facts; sports; Did You Know?; more action; has cartoons on the cover; has fighting figures; mostly boys in it;

Total Girl—more happy people; lots of celebrities; more about pop stars; articles about lip gloss; famous girls on the cover: girls on the front cover are "pretty hot"; article about learning how to dance; only girls in it;

Design Features;

Total Girl—real photos; squares have round corners; soft-looking girls;

K-Zone—sharp, angular corners; action figures.

During this work session Fiona and I could not help but notice how engaged the children were; all groups worked industriously. At the end of the session Fiona complimented

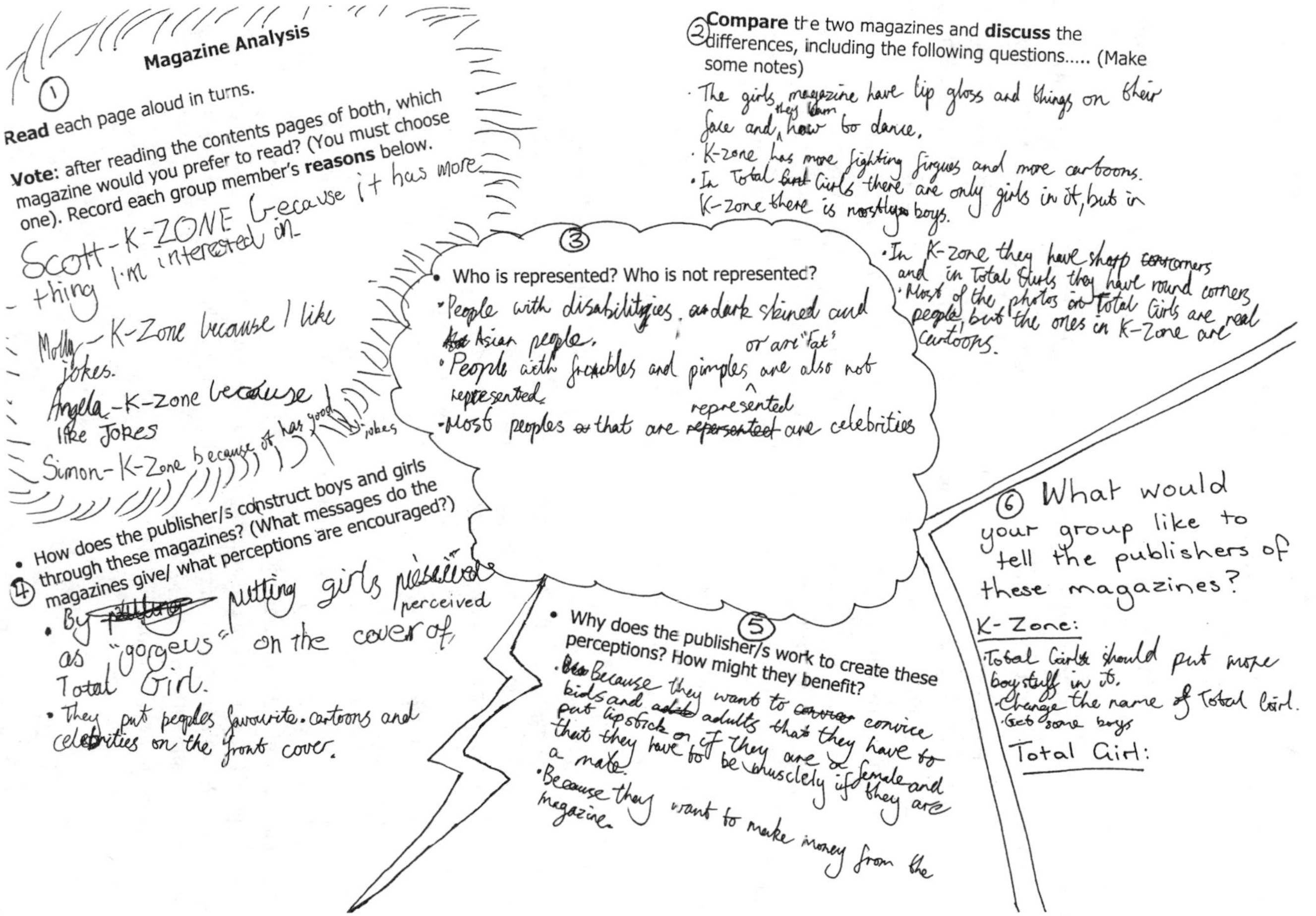
Magazine Analysis
1
Read each page aloud in turns.
Vote: after reading the contents pages of both, which magazine would you prefer to read? (You must choose one). Record each group member's reasons below.
Scott - K-ZONE because it has more thing I'm interested in.
Molly - K-Zone because I like jokes.
Angela - K-zone because I like Jokes
Simon - K-Zone because of has good jokes
2 Compare the two magazines and discuss the differences, including the following questions..... (Make some notes)
· The girls magazine have lip gloss and things on their face and they learn how to dance.
· K-zone has more fighting figures and more cartoons.
· In Total Girls there are only girls in it, but in K-zone there is mostly boys.
· In K-zone they have sharp corners and in Total Girls they have round corners.
· Most of the photos on Total Girls are real people but the ones in K-Zone are cartoons.
3
• Who is represented? Who is not represented?
· People with disabilities, dark skined and Asian people.
· People with freckles and pimples or are "fat" are also not represented.
· Most peoples that are represented are celebrities
• How does the publisher/s construct boys and girls through these magazines? (What messages do the magazines give/ what perceptions are encouraged?)
4
• By putting girls perceived as "gorgeus" on the cover of Total Girl.
• They put peoples favourite cartoons and celebrities on the front cover.
5
• Why does the publisher/s work to create these perceptions? How might they benefit?
· Because they want to convice kids and adults that they have to put lipstick on if they are a female and that they have to be muscley if they are a male.
· Because they want to make money from the magazine.
6 What would your group like to tell the publishers of these magazines?
K-Zone:
· Total Girls should put more boy stuff in it.
· Change the name of Total Girl.
· Get some boys
Total Girl:

Figure 2–1

the children on how they had worked in their groups. She asked them to tell us why they had been so involved. Here are just three of their responses:

> The subject was really cool.
>
> Reading magazine pages is what we like to do.
>
> It was new and different work.

This is a reminder of the importance of making links between the children's in-school and out-of-school lives.

Session 2   The session started with a general class sharing of what had happened in the first session. Some children talked about the stereotyping of girls in the *Total Girl* magazine. Others pointed out that while there were no boys in the *Total Girl* magazines there were one or two girls in *K-Zone*. The children continued with their group work.

Individually the children were challenged to write to the publisher of the magazines regarding the construction of gender. Importantly here, the children were taking action. They were not passive spectators but, rather, active participants challenging the publisher about perceived stereotypes. The children's letters to the publisher included their addresses and surnames but they have beeen removed here for privacy.

> *12/12/03*
> *Dear Publisher,*
>   *My name is Tanya and I am concerned about some of the messages you give in your magazine,* Total Girl.
>   *Why are there always pretty people in magazines, not people in wheelchairs? Why are there so many famous stars in magazines? Why aren't kids chosen from schools? Why do boys have to look rough and girls have to look nice?*
>   *I would be happier if there was a magazine published for both boys and girls. It would be great to see different children, like tomboys, kids in hospitals, etc. in these magazines. This would mean that people wouldn't be left out.*
> *Yours Sincerely*
> *Tanya*
>
> *12/12/03*
> *Dear Publisher of* Total Girl *and* K-Zone *Magazines,*
> *I am disgusted at how you're constructing children to stay in all-girl & all-boy groups.*
>   *In the 19th century people may of thought it was the right thing, not now it's the 21st century and children should decide themselves.*
>   *It's wrong to decide for the kids what boys should and girls should play with.*
> *Yours Truly*
> *Corey*
>
> *12/12/03*
> *Dear Publishers of* Total Girl,
> *I am a student at Moonee Ponds West Primary School and I am writing to you after having a session at school on your magazines.*

> *After looking at a few of your magazines, I am truly disgusted at what you have on the front and through your mag.*
>
> *Being a blonde haired girl and light skinned who doesn't like the color pink and playing with dolls, I am really offended when reading in your magazine, which is full of soft colors and light haired girls.*
>
> *Where are the dark skinned people or dark haired girls in the mag or front cover?*
>
> *Who gives you the right to just put what is perceived as beautiful and blond haired girls in your mag?*
>
> *This is giving girls of today an image that they need to fit in and if they don't then according to your magazine they're not normal.*
>
> *So please consider having different people in your magazine.*
>
> *Thanks lots!*
>
> *Emma*

Linguistic Analysis of Magazine Editorial: What's Wrong with This Country?

Critical literacy includes the quite-specific study of how writers use language to construct particular representations. An editorial from *Cigar Aficionado: The Good Life Magazine for Men*, was used to introduce some grade 4–5–6 children to simple linguistic analysis. The editorial ranted about the draconian government regulations that grouped cigar smokers with smokers of cigarettes. It painted a very repressed lifestyle for today's smokers.

I told the children the article we were going to read was from a magazine published in the United States. The editorial title was written large for all to see—"What's Wrong with This Country?" The children were asked to predict what the article would be about. The children's names were included with their statements on the classroom list.

some problems with the country

how we could make it better

war and terrorism

people getting too fat in America

positives and negatives about America

crimes

The children were each given a copy of the editorial to read. Later, I scribed on a large chart statements from the children telling what the article was about:

not being allowed to smoke cigars and cigarettes

fighting for the right to smoke cigars in public places

smuggling cigarettes into their houses to smoke them

looking at the smokers' side

The children were asked to think who the writers of the article might be. They agreed quite quickly the writers would be cigar smokers. (Later in the lesson they began to verbalize that the editors might manufacture and make money from selling cigars and may not actually smoke them.) I then showed the children the magazine and gave them the title, *Cigar Aficionado*.

It was explained to the students that we were going to analyze or look very closely at how the writers had constructed, firstly, the government officials and secondly, the smokers, by identifying the groups of words or phrases that described the actions of both groups; that is, the verb phrases. With the children following along in their copies of the editorial, we identified together some of the actions of government. The children underlined these. Then working in pairs the children continued finding the verb phrases for both groups—government officials and smokers. From the children's work a class list was compiled.

Government Officials
have banned smoking
prohibit the U.S. postal service from shipping tobacco products by mail
[mayor of New York] condoned his buddies' law-breaking activity
imposing draconian laws that prohibit smoking
have tried to find every possible way to lump cigars together with cigarettes
[mayor] exibited an outrageous degree of hypocrisy
eliminate all chance to smoke in public

Smokers
being trampled on
are simply ignored
forced to use expensive mail services
wouldn't have been able to shop by catalogue, order by phone or Internet
braving cold and rain
hang their heads out windows

The children were asked to silently read each of the above lists and think how the writers were constructing both the governments and smokers. I scribed their comments:

Construction of Governments
all negative
power crazy
not thinking of the smokers
really strict
only thinking of their side

not nice

being unfair

Construction of Smokers

the good guys (I asked the child who gave this response to read out the verb phrases or descriptions of smoker actions that implied they were good guys. He could not find any and so changed his statement to the one that appears next.)

being treated like dirt

they're victims

forced to do stuff against their will

innocent

they're the ones suffering

no one cares about them

Next we listed the groups whose opinions were missing in this article:

nonsmokers

governments (they've just been written about)

cigarette smokers

ex-smokers

children

restaurant and pub owners (smoking drives their clients away)

workers in restaurants and pubs

passive smokers

doctors and scientists

The children were next asked to rewrite or to transform the first few paragraphs of the editorial changing the construction of governments and smokers. Here are some of the children's responses.

What's Right About This Country?

It really makes sense what this country is doing—banning smoking in all public restaurants and bars.

The smokers might get sick of being out in the cold and rain and end up not winning and quit. That would make this a fantastic country.

Non-smokers love to be able to go out and have a smoke free night—just what they wanted.

Maybe smokers will get sick of being ignored and having to pay so much to get a packet of cigars.

Maybe soon no-one will smoke and our country won't be polluted.

—ISABELLE, GRADE 6

Bar Tender

Any of you enjoy the Super Bowl? Well not me. Every day I go to work I'm surrounded by cigarette smoke. It's just outrageous. I wish I lived in Florida, Massachusetts, California or New York. They're in luck. Smoking is banned in almost all indoor places there.

The good thing is the government is spreading the law around to different states. It would be great to be able to work where the smokers have to smoke outside and I wouldn't have to worry about getting cancer.

This country is finally going in the right direction. It makes sense.

—LUKE, GRADE 6

What's Right Within This Country (The Government Perspective)

The non-smokers that went and partied after the Super Bowl enjoyed a smoke free night in the local bars and restaurants. The Government believes that the State of America that have banned smoking have done the right thing and are hopeful that by taking away smoking cigars and cigarettes, will reduce deaths in America caused by smoking. The smokers may believe that this new law is unfair—they should take a look at the workers in bars and restaurants who have to breathe in their bad smoking habits. The Government will fight against the smokers. They may fight back but the Government will fight harder.

—SUSIE, GRADE 6

Linguistic Analysis of Newspaper and Magazine Articles: Australian Idol

Australian Idol, a television program that seeks to create a new Australian pop star, is part of the International Idol television extravaganza, where each national winner competes to be the International Pop Idol.

Several months ago one of the Australian judges attracted criticism from the Australian public and the media for his attack on one of the contestants regarding his body shape. This became the substance of some critical literacy work in Shirl Ramage and Annie Drennan's grade 4–5–6. The focus was body image and the construction of pop stars.

Session 1   The session began with a discussion of the *Australian Idol* program. A show of hands indicated that of the fifty-four students in the group, only four had never watched the program. Some of their classmates explained to these four what happened on this particular program. The issue of a recent furor about one judge's attack on a contestant, Courtney's, body shape was raised. The children were all very familiar with this, and some had strong opinions about it.

Each child was given a copy of a newspaper article entitled, "Is This Man Too Fat to Be a Pop Star?" The children read the article. In response to the article, the children wrote their opinions on the issue, in the subgenre of argument (Text participant: Luke/Freebody 1999).

Is this man too fat to be a pop star?

My opinion is that as long as Courtney sings well then Ian Dickson should leave him and his weight alone. One of the major reasons I think this, is because Dicko is the one who always raves on about the way he wants someone who can sell records, so why does his image matter? I doubt people are going to walk into Sanity and say "I like this guy's voice but he's fat so I don't want to buy his CD."

Another reason is since his unofficial nick-name is "the fat guy," so now it's his brand, just like Guy Sebastian's afro and Shannon Noll's goatee beard. It gets him to be noticed.

I think the media have gone over the top though. There is much worse things happening in the world than a guy being called fat!

—DANIEL

Is this man too fat to be a pop star?

If Ian Dickson said that comment in concern about his heart and fitness, then yes, I do agree with him.

I think our Australian Idol needs to have a good personality, a good style of music and of course, a good voice. I think Courtney has got all of that and mostly everyone loves him so much.

Also if he loses weight for health problems, then I agree with Dicko, but if it's just for looks, I strongly disagree.

—KELLY

Is this man too fat to be a pop star?

I don't agree with Ian Dickson's comments that Australian Idol's Courtney Murphy is too fat to be a pop star.

I think that if somebody has a brilliant voice that it shouldn't matter whether they have a differen't body shape, to what is stereotyped of how a musician/pop star should look. Just because Britney Spears and other pop stars like her, have good bodies, doesn't mean every pop star/ musician has to look like them. Also it will put people that are bigger than everyone else, or have a different body shape, off a career in singing even if they do have wonderful singing voices, because of Ian Dickson's comments, that the industry won't accept people who are different.

In conclusion I say that Courtney has done extremely well to get as far as he has in Australian Idol. He is now in the top six and I give him congratulations for getting that far.

—ELISE

Is this man too fat to be a pop star?

I don't think he's too fat because he must have a good voice. When you listen to a CD you listen to the music. You don't watch them, you listen.

Also if he's not unhealthy fat, that's OK. He's not sick or unwell because of it. The show is a singing contest. I think Dicko should get off Courtney's back.

—STUART

Is this man too fat to be a pop star?

Courtney is not too fat to be a pop star. It doesn't matter whether your fat, thin, boy or girl, what really matters is how good your voice is. That's what the competition is about.

There are other people (not naming names) that are a bit bulky too. Why doesn't Dicko comment about them? Just because Courtney is a little bit bigger than other, Dickson has to comment.

Last year Dicko said Paulini was too fat for her dress. She wasn't. Is Dicko obsessed with weight or is he just trying to pick on good singers eg Courtney, Paulini, Ricky-Lee, to make people give them less votes to make the competition more interesting?

I think Courtney has one of the best voices in the competition. Who cares what he looks like, He's got a great personality and voice which is what matters. It's what's on the inside that matters.

In conclusion I would just like to say Courtney is not fat but one thing he is, is a good singer with a great personality.

—Lauren

At the conclusion of this discussion, the children shared those talents they believed important for success as a pop singer. (Children who had finished earlier than others with their written opinion had individually listed necessary talents for being successful pop stars.) A class list was compiled.

outgoing performer

crowd worker

versatile singer

mover and groover

passionate singer

confident performer

dancing sensation

spirited singer

superb mover

audience connector

golden-voiced singer

talented entertainer

Session 2: Deconstruction of Text   Each child reread the article and underlined all the groups of words or individual words that stood in place of "Courtney." In other words, the children were asked to underline all noun phrases referring to Courtney. A class list of these noun phrases was then compiled from the children's lists.

bulky Australian Idol singer

24-year-old performer from Perth

he

the big guy

the fat guy

The children discussed how none of these terms gave any information about Courtney's astounding entertaining abilities.

   The class read "Idols' Winning Hints," in *Idols Party* magazine (2004, 6–7). This
article had nothing to do with the issue of Courtney's body shape but was published at
the same time. It consisted of interview responses from each 2003 National Idol winner, with tips for winning a national pop contest. Working in pairs, the children underlined all the words these successful pop stars used to describe what it is that aspiring
stars need to do to get to the top in the pop industry. That is, the children underlined
all the verb phrases. The class compiled a list from the children's lists.

> avoid smoky places
> don't be lazy
> push yourself
> be yourself
> need a good voice
> believe in yourself
> live for music
> don't let it go to your head
> work hard
> don't try to be cool
> be on the same level as those listening
> put some emotion into songs
> be yourself
> be versatile with range of songs
> be talented and very disciplined
> believe singing is only thing you can do

The children then studied the two class lists: one list of noun phrases from the newspaper article reporting a judge's comments; and the other list of verb phrases from the
"Idols' Winning Hints" article. The children summed up the construction of a successful pop star from each of these lists; for example, from the judge's comments list: A pop
star has to be slim and look good, and from the idols' winning tips list: To be the
Australian Idol it is important to be yourself, to work hard, and to believe in yourself.
The children noted that the winning competitors did not mention body image, except
for the World Winner, who stated it did not worry him what he looked like.

Sessions 3 and 4   The children each made a large poster of Courtney performing (Figures 2–2, 2–3, 2–4, and 2–5). When the artwork was completed, they added two captions. One caption was to reflect the values of the judge, and the second was to describe
Courtney as a performer focusing on his performing skills.

Session 5: Action   Children were given choices. They could write either to Courtney,
the competitor; or to the producer of *Australian Idol*; or to Ian Dickson, the judge, to
express their points of view.

Figure 2–2

Figure 2–3

Figure 2–4

Figure 2–5

Class Listing of Critical Literacy Strategies

In the same way teachers explicitly talk with young readers about the strategies they might use when they are reading as code breakers (Luke and Freebody 1999) and list these strategies in their classrooms, so children can identify what it is they do when they read and write critically. Here are ideas pooled by children in a grade 5–6 class to answer the question, What is critical literacy?

> **Critical Literacy**
>
> When a person writes to attract attention or a different point of view.
>
> Not to believe everything you read.
>
> A reader thinks about an article differently.
>
> The act of recognizing how an author tries to manipulate the reader by the language used.
>
> To analyze text.
>
> To develop skills to think of what the text really means.
>
> Text that manipulates the reader into believing what the author wants.

Lists like these are alive. They are referred to regularly. The children are free to revise their earlier statements and to add new ones. When you read these lists you may query one or two statements and say, "But that is not critical literacy." What is important is that all children feel free to have a go, to say what they think, not what they think the teacher wants to hear. Only when children are honest about what they perceive (in this example) critical literacy to be, is the teacher informed of the children's current understandings; she knows where more teaching is needed.

Summary: Critical Literacy

If school programs are working toward a worldview of social justice and participatory democracy, critical literacy is an essential part of the literacy curriculum. This includes teaching concepts basic to a study of social justice, and teaching strategies that enable students to deconstruct texts and carefully analyze decisions made by the creators in the construction of the text that position particular groups of people in particular ways. Building on this work, students can critically analyze their own representations of social groups in the texts they write. And, by transforming or challenging the perspectives and stereotypes identified in public texts, they take action.

References

Christensen, L. 1999. "Critical Literacy: Teaching Reading, Writing and Outrage." In *Making Justice Our Project,* edited by C. Edelsky. Urbana, IL: NCTE.

Durrant, C., and B. Green. 2000. "Literacy and the New Technologies in School Education: Meeting the L(IT)eracy Challenge?"*The Australian Journal of Language and Literacy*, 23 (2): 89–108.

Herman, E. S. 1992. *Beyond Hypocrisy: Decoding the News in an Age of Propaganda Including the Doublespeak Dictionary*. Boston: South End Press.

Luke, A., and P. Freebody. 1999. "A Map of Possible Practices: Further Notes on the Four Resources Model." *Practically Primary*, 4 (2): 5–8.

Luke, A., J. O'Brien, and B. Comber. 2001. "Making Community Texts Objects of Study." In *Critical Literacy: A Collection of Articles from the Australian Literacy Educators Association*, edited by H. Fehring and P. Green. Delaware, MD, and Adelaide, South Australia: IRA and ALEA.

Lukin, A. 2003. "The Power of Language." ABC Broadcast, Sunday, March 16.

Pitt, J. 1995. *Not Just After Lunch on Wednesdays. Critical Literacy: A Personal View*. Department for Education and Children's Services, South Australia.

Wilson, L. 1997. "Defining Whole Language in a Postmodern Age." *The Australian Journal of Language and Learning*, 20 (2): 116–30.

———. 2002. *Reading to Live: How to Teach Reading for Today's World*. Portsmouth, NH: Heinemann.

Children's Books

Crew, G., and G. Rogers. 1992. *Tracks*. Melbourne: Lothian Books.

Crew, G., and S. Wollman. 1994. *The WaterTower*. South Australia, Martin International Pty Ltd. in association with ERA publications.

Jorgensen, N., and B. Harrison-Lever. 2002, *In Flanders Fields*. Fremantle, Western Australia: Sandcastle Books, Fremantle Arts Centre Press.

Magazines

"Idols Winning Hints." 2004. *Idols Party*, no. 5, 6–7.

"What's Wrong with This Country?" 2004. *Cigar Aficionado: The Good Life Magazine for Men*, 12 (3): 7.

TV Hits. 2001. Pacific Publications Pty Ltd. August (156), 35–51.

Children's Magazines

K-Zone, Pacific Publications, McMahons Point, New South Wales.

Total Girl, Pacific Publications, McMahons Point, New South Wales.

CHAPTER 3

WRITING AS SOCIAL PRACTICE

My Dad Says

My dad says . . .
    School's a bludge
    No homework
    No spelling tests
    No tables to learn
    Too much fun
    Too many excursions
    Too many camps.

He says
    There's not enough work.

Not enough work!
    I had to keep a camp diary.
    I wrote the camp song.
    I balanced the camp budget.
    I published the camp report.

Yes. School is fun.

—LORRAINE WILSON

In the big wide world, writing is not an end in itself. Writing accompanies and is part of daily social practices. We write a shopping list of the groceries we need at the supermarket. We write a curriculum vitae when making application for a new job. Making a plan for the house of our dreams involves writing. Taking the minutes of a meeting involves writing. Writing in a personal diary involves writing. Keeping score at cricket involves writing. Some families exchange messages with their children in the form of notes attached by magnets to the fridge door. Emailing our friends in cyberspace or joining in a conversation on a chat line involves writing. Interestingly, chatting now is writing! For the younger generation, leaving text messages on mobile phones involves writing, be it done with thumb rather than pen. When understanding the link between language and social practice we speak of discourses. Discourses are ways of valuing, behaving, and using language assumed by particular groups of people as they engage in particular activities. So a social practice assumes more than a particular way of using language; it assumes ways of dressing, of feeling, of behaving. James Gee has said

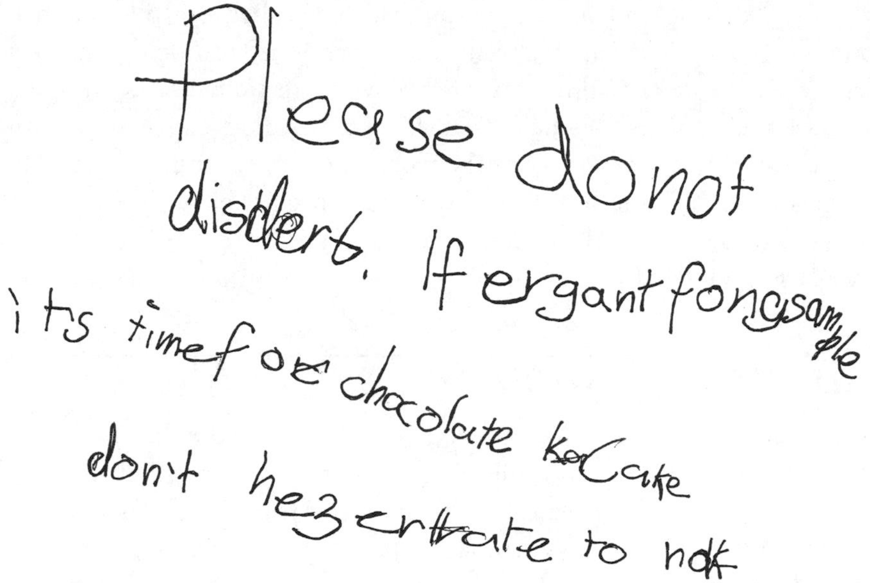

Figure 3–1

discourses "are always and everywhere social. Language as well as literacy, is always and everywhere integrated with, and relative to social practices constituting particular discourses" (1990, xv–xxi). If one wishes to join a yacht club and become a sailor it is not enough to learn the language of sailing. One has to wear appropriate clothing and engage in particular activities necessary for the smooth sailing of the yacht.

On any day each one of us engages in life practices accompanied by related language and literacy practices. So too with children. Sam and Eleanor, age seven and eight, shut themselves in their bedroom one afternoon after pinning the following note to the bedroom door (see Figure 3–1): "Please do not disturb. If urgent for example it's time for chocolate cake don't hesitate to knock. Sam and Eleanor" Note how confident these young siblings are in using writing to exert some power in their household.

In another example, a friend of mine was driving her grandchildren, who were in the back seat of her car. Hannah, age seven, was looking at street directory, Hugh, age five, said, "Is that a map of Melbourne?" My friend replied from the front seat, "It is not one map of Melbourne. There are many maps that show all the suburbs and all the streets in Melbourne."

HANNAH: Is Hopetoun St in here? [Hopetoun is the street where Hannah and her family live.]
GRANDMOTHER: Yes. But I can't find it for you right now. If you turn to the back you will find it listed under letter "H." Next to it will be the page number and grid references to help you find Hopetoun Street.

My friend kept driving, but in a short time Hannah called out that she had found Hopetoun Street. Later she was able to show my friend the location of the street on the directory. I am not sure of Hannah's experience with street directories but I'm sure she must have seen her parents use one to find where they were going. A street directory is an authentic world text. Hannah knew the name of her street and somehow she found it on the page. As Frank Smith has said, "Children have to behave like language users, to share the purpose for which the language is being used, in order to learn how the language is used" (1984, 150).

Authentic Classroom Writing

In classrooms a multitude of daily practices are accompanied by writing. The school grounds are to be upgraded. The children sketch and make notes of the playground they desire. They submit their plans to the school governing body. They write up their ideas for publication in the school newsletter, which goes home to parents.

After experiments with magnets, the children write all they have learned so they can make a book to read to the class next door.

A book-launch of books published by the children is to be held. The children write invitations to family members, inviting them to attend. Writing is integral to life practices.

When one sees that writing is not an end in itself, one appreciates the part played by writing in all subject areas. Children write to hypothesize, to plan, to report on and conclude about scientific understandings. They write to plan social investigations and surveys, they draft questions for interviews, they write letters seeking information, and later they write to collate the data they gather.

If children are to value writing; if they are to come to know that writing is integral to many life activities then they must see connections between their lives and writing. Having children sit silently each day completing grammar exercises or spelling exercises in workbooks does not endear them to writing, nor does it teach them the benefits of writing for enriching their lives. Only when the writing curriculum of the classroom relates to the children, their families, their hobbies, their communities; only when it serves authentic purposes for them, will they engage with and value writing. Only then will they develop confidence in themselves as writers in a wide range of life activities; only then will they be strong enough to use their writing to protest injustice and to write for change.

Multiple Literacies

Allied to this view of literacy as social practice is the notion of multiple literacies. To live and function at this particular time one engages with different literacies. Think of electronic literacies. I write the manuscript for this book on a computer powered by electricity. I can now communicate with someone overseas via email, by typing on a computer keyboard—again, powered by electricity. By clicking one icon on the screen with the use of a mouse one can send that communication anywhere in the world, so long as the recipient is connected to email. No paper is used; no pen, no quill. No middle person such as a postman or UPS driver is needed to help ensure that the communication reaches the recipient. In reality, I guess the service provider has become the middle man.

To access a Web page one needs to understand all sorts of icons on the computer screen and to be prepared to work in directions other than left to right and progressively down a page. The eye scans the screen, like the movements of a firefly darting through the evening air. Web pages offer many alternate pathways, unlike the novel I read of an evening, which flows in one linear direction.

With email we still spell words in full as we did in written communications fifty to one hundred years ago, although some word spellings may have changed. Contrast the written communications sent via the computer with those sent on the mobile phone. Because of the minute screen space, the language is extremely abbreviated. As with email, no pen or paper is used. A generation ago, who would have envisaged the thumb as writing implement! One wonders about the evolutionary change in the shape of the human thumb, with the speed and dexterity now observed in sending text messages. I observe young people's thumbs move with incredible speed and considerable dexterity as they type on their phones. When I try to read their phones I am illiterate. A whole new language is being developed and used by mobile phone users. Consider the following:

LOL	laughing out loud
SIT	stay in touch
TIC	tongue in cheek
TTUL	talk to you later
<Y>	yawning
<S>	smiling
3sum	threesome

—From WAN2TLK? Ltle bk of txt msgs (2000)

Fifth- and sixth-grade classrooms could well have those students with mobile phones record the language of text messages on a chart or in a book for the benefit of other students just learning about text messages. They are the experts in this new literacy.

Young students today play numerous electronic games and subscribe to magazines that assist in the playing of these games. When I attempt to read the N64 magazines, as with text messages, I again see quite abbreviated language where a letter equals a word. Not only older students but also very young students are practicing literacies not used in classrooms, with considerable skill.

Young children developing initial literacy knowledge and skills in homes where Internet access and CD-ROMS are available, develop skills appropriate to these particular conditions and requirements. They learn to "read" these texts in the most effective ways possible. These are not necessarily the same skills and knowledge that accompany linear print-based texts. (Carrington 2001, 96)

These new literacies have developed as people have used new communication tools as part of daily life routines. It is a humbling lesson to those of us from older generations to find that in the company of our grandchildren, some are more literate than we are with certain types of modern texts. Not having a mobile phone I am absolutely at a loss when presented with a text message! Of concern in relation to the new electronic literacies is the exclusion of some families, for economic reasons. Computers are so much more expensive than pens and paper. It hardly seems fair that some children have their very own computers in their very own bedrooms, while others do not have enough food, let alone a single computer, in their home. In the future, economic factors may be a bigger determinant than ever before in who succeeds in school. Classrooms must keep pace with the times. Classrooms must keep pace with student lives. What are the new literacies? What are the literacies students practice outside school hours? Today, in planning for children's development in literacy, we must plan for the new literacies so important in the lives of young people and in the education and business fields. To survive in today's world we need more than the literacy of pen and paper, using conventionally spelled words in lines from left to right across a page.

How Are New Literacies Learned?

In a book about children learning to write it is timely to stop and reflect how we adults have learned some of the new literacies. Think for a moment about how you became proficient in using email. Did you attend lessons? Most probably not. How, then, did we learn? The starting point for me, and I guess for most people, was need: in my work situation colleagues were expecting me to have an email address. Different committees used email to contact members and it was extra work for the secretaries to post or fax separately to those without email addresses. Those without email were seen as akin to living with the dinosaurs. Once I had a modem and service provider, it was a matter of demonstrations from friends and much trial and error, in learning to use email. How important friends were at the end of phone lines, to get me out of trouble or to solve some new problem. How many mistakes I made. We see here the application of Cambourne's (1988) conditions of learning to the process of older learners acquiring a new literacy. As we learn to email, we are immersed in what email is through incoming emails; friends demonstrate what to do; we are thoroughly engaged because it is imperative we become competent to survive in our professional fields; we engage in regular use, opening the emails each morning and replying; our learning involves making mistakes or approximations; the responsibility for the order in which we acquire the necessary skills and technical knowledge is left to us; our colleagues expect that we will master emailing, no one is expected to fail; our friends respond to our requests for help at the point of need.

We learn to be proficient in using email as we use it for life purposes, that is, as social practice. I needed to learn how to email to be a proper functioning member of various committees. I needed to learn to email to be a participant on list servs.

It is interesting to reflect how the language and structure of email messages has evolved. When I commenced emailing I began with "Dear . . ." So did others emailing me. No one does that now. Sometimes the recipient's name is not even stated. It is assumed if the email has been sent to someone's email address that person will read the mail and thus it is superfluous to add a name. (This never applied to snail mail.) The literacy of emails has evolved and is evolving as we learn to use it.

It is salient for teachers who are learning new literacies to reflect on how they are learning, and how important are kindly responses at the point of need, for this is what their students are experiencing as they learn to write.

Children Explain Their Literacies

One way of persuading students that classroom life is an extension of the world outside is to invite them to bring their literacies into the classroom. I invited Shirl Ramage and Annie Drennan's grade 5–6 children to teach me their literacies. I could tell by the looks on their faces when I first said this that they thought I was putting them on; how could a teacher not be able to read or write something they could? When I explained that, for example, I did not have a mobile phone and that I had never ever seen a text message, let alone read one, they began to understand. Over the next few weeks, the students' task was to teach me and others who did not use their texts how to read them. Some children explained different sports score systems, some explained electronic game language, and Jonathan set out to explain how to use a mobile phone for the purpose of sending and receiving text messages. All of the children's first drafts assumed knowledge about the controls or symbols that some of us did not have. When individuals shared, all students were asked to question when they could not understand or "read" the literacy being explained. Jonathan, for example, in his first presentation had written that to spell "Hello" on his mobile phone, one pressed "h" and then "e" and so on. He was a little taken aback when I asked, "Where does one find letter 'h' on a phone?" His completed draft includes much more detail (Figures 3–2, 3–3, and 3–4).

Authentic Writing as Part of Classroom Integrated Programs

The understanding that writing is not an end in itself but rather accompanies some life practice or life event means that texts in classrooms should be authentic; they are necessary for participation in particular practices. I outline now in detail how one particular text type was introduced because it was essential to the class social investigation.

Examples of using S.M.S.

I would like to spell "**Hello**".

TIP: IF THE LETTER THAT YOU WANT IS THE FIRST LETTER ON THAT KEY PRESS ONCE
IF IT IS SECOND PRESS THE KEY TWICE IF IT IS THIRD PRESS IT THREE TIMES.

> Press 4 two times for H.
> Press 3 two times for E.
> .Press 5 three times for L.

Then wait until the flashing line moves across because if the letter that
you
want is on the same number the phone will go through the punctuation or
the
letter that is after it.

> Press 5 three times for L.
> Press 6 three times for O.

IF YOU WANT TO USE PUNCTUATION PRESS ✳ THEN
CHOOSE THE PUNCTUATION THAT YOU WANT. MAKE SURE
THAT THE FLASHING LINE IS WERE YOU WANT THE
PUNCTUATION.

Some short cuts for words and messages.

You=U.	Please=Pls
Are=R.	Okay=O.K
why=?.	Today=2day
What=Wat.	Tomorrow=2morow.
Hello=Hi.	Tonight=2nite
To=2.	Tea/Dinner=T
Your=Ur.	
For=4.	Afternoon=Arvo.
See=C.	Morning=Morn.
Be=B.	Love=Luv.
Would=Wud.	Wouldn't=Wudnt.
Could=Cud.	Couldn't=Cudnt.
Should=Shud.	Shouldn't=Shudnt.
Through=Thru.	

Time Saver: When you get into the messages menu scroll through to
templates you Will find Time consuming messages for example:
("Please call").Press the read button then press options and sending options
will come up.
If it has got(......)that means there is more to that template.

To changes
letters to
Capitals or
Lower case.

Figure 3–2   Jonathan's Mobile Phone Explanation

Pen-Pal Letters

Vicki McCormack and Helen Lockart team-teach a K–2 group of forty-two children. They wanted to ensure that the rights and responsibilities developed in their classroom community be extended to the children's behavior beyond the school, so they planned an extended study about friendship and relationships between people, which they called

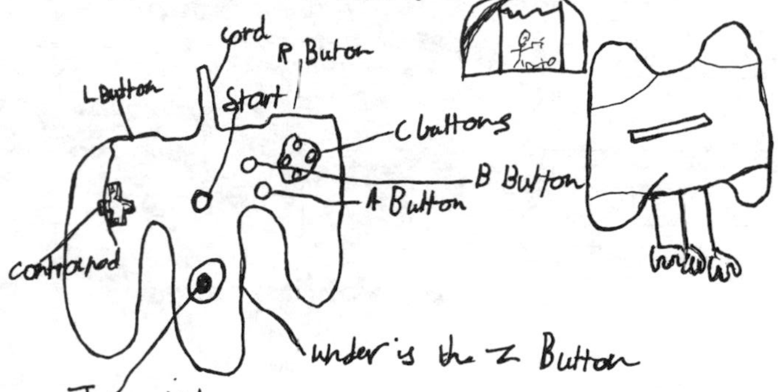

Figure 3–3 Rhys Explains the Controls of a N64 Game

L Brorers Rhys

N64
Buttons
Fup, C down, C right, C left, A, B, R, L, Z,
Joy stick control pad.

Controls for James Bond

A change weapon, B Reload, Round L
A arm Z, Fire Trigger, C left do a
sharp left run, C Right do a right
sharp Run, C down keeping C up
enhance armer
Joy stick Move Point gun up and down
control pad
while not aiming
Start Menuu selection

cord
R Button
Start
C buttons
B Button
A Button
L Button
control pad
Joy stick
where's the z Button

Aditional things you can get Controler Pact.
Transphure pack, Expansion pack, Rumple,

Rhys

enables you to save a game.
A transfer pack lets you put game boy
games in the controler and put game boy
it on the TV. The Expansion pack!
Lts you get if there is
a game with a secong one series you
can unlock if with an Expansion pack
with a rumble jack if something impacts
in the game your controler shakes

Put youre finger first
of youre left hand on the
Z button then put youre
left thumb on the joy stick
then put your right thumb
on the A button and
the first finger on the R button
then if the other buttons are right
need you rotate first to
press the buttons youre first to

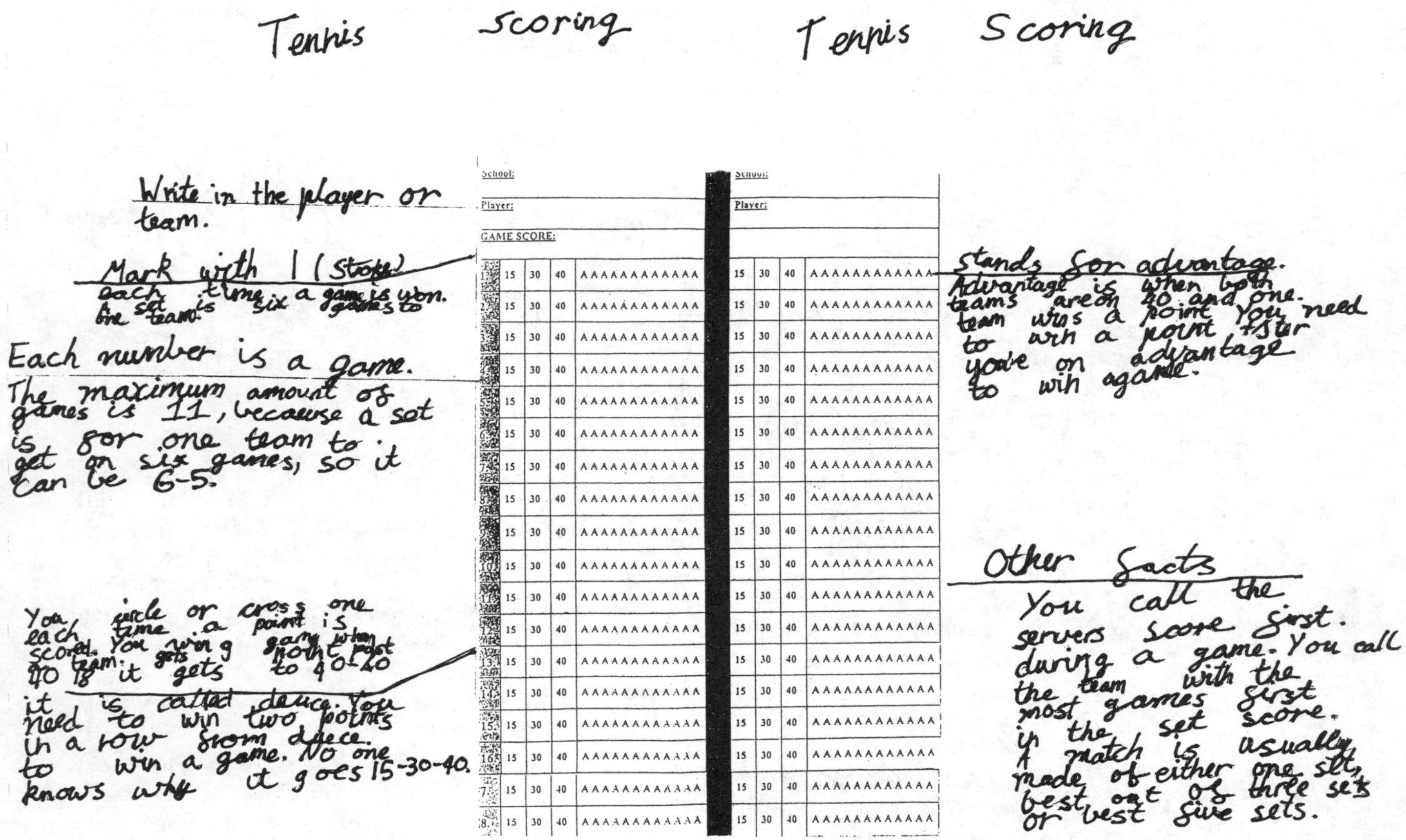

Tennis Scoring

Write in the player or team.

Mark with 1 (stop) each time a team wins a game's upon the team's team.

Each number is a game.

The maximum amount of games is 11, because a set is for one team to get six games, so it can be 6-5.

You circle or cross one each time a point is scored. You win a point to begin it gets to go 0 to 20. It is called deuce points. Need to win two from there. In a row from deuce. To win a game. No one knows why it goes 15-30-40.

Stands for advantage. Advantage is when both teams are 40 point. You need team who's to win with a point after you're on with a advantage. to with advantage.

Other facts

You call the servers score first. score a game. You all during with the first the team games most set score. in the set usually. if match is made of either the side best out of three sets. or last five sets.

GAME SCORE:						School:					
Player:						Player:					
15	30	40	AAAAAAAAAA			15	30	40	AAAAAAAAAA		
15	30	40	AAAAAAAAAA			15	30	40	AAAAAAAAAA		
15	30	40	AAAAAAAAAA			15	30	40	AAAAAAAAAA		
15	30	40	AAAAAAAAAA			15	30	40	AAAAAAAAAA		
15	30	40	AAAAAAAAAA			15	30	40	AAAAAAAAAA		
15	30	40	AAAAAAAAAA			15	30	40	AAAAAAAAAA		
15	30	40	AAAAAAAAAA			15	30	40	AAAAAAAAAA		
15	30	40	AAAAAAAAAA			15	30	40	AAAAAAAAAA		
15	30	40	AAAAAAAAAA			15	30	40	AAAAAAAAAA		
15	30	40	AAAAAAAAAA			15	30	40	AAAAAAAAAA		
15	30	40	AAAAAAAAAA			15	30	40	AAAAAAAAAA		
15	30	40	AAAAAAAAAA			15	30	40	AAAAAAAAAA		
15	30	40	AAAAAAAAAA			15	30	40	AAAAAAAAAA		
15	30	40	AAAAAAAAAA			15	30	40	AAAAAAAAAA		
15	30	40	AAAAAAAAAA			15	30	40	AAAAAAAAAA		
15	30	40	AAAAAAAAAA			15	30	40	AAAAAAAAAA		

Figure 3–4   Chris Explains How to Read a Tennis Score Sheet

We're All in This Together. A short distance from their school is a neighboring school with a very diverse student population. Vicki and Helen's students are, on the whole, from middle-class families with a few newly arrived migrant children. At Ascot Vale West Primary School nearby, the student population includes many who live in public housing, including newly arrived immigrant children from African nations, some of whom are Muslim. The two teachers negotiated with a friend teaching at Ascot Vale West Primary School to set up a pen-pal program between the two schools with the intention of having the children meet. Two grade 1–2 classes exchanged pen-pal letters with the children from Vicki and Helen's double K–2. The Moonee Ponds West K–2 children drew the names of the Ascot Vale West children from a hat to determine their pen pals. Vicki and Helen then demonstrated letter writing. They explicitly introduced the address and date at the top of the letter, the greeting to the recipient, and at the end, the signature of the writer. The children then wrote letters to their pen pals. When they conferenced, the teachers focused first on the content and then on the form of the letter. Later, the letters were mailed to Ascot Vale West Primary School. Figures 3–5 and 3–6 show first-draft letters from Greta and Imogen. Their redrafted letters went in the mail.

Note how six-year-old Imogen begins by checking whether Jayme is a boy or a girl. Imogen's mother told me how exciting the pen-pal project was to Imogen. In the lead-up to the day the children met, Imogen was counting the hours until she met her new friend.

After several letters were exchanged, the Ascot Vale West teachers had each of their students individually write a "Who Am I" about themselves, to send to their pen pals. In the "Who Am I" the children only included information they had written in their earlier letters. The "Who Am I's" were mailed to Moonee Ponds West together with a name label and a photograph of each Ascot Vale West child except for several Somali girls, who were not allowed to be photographed. The task for Vicki and Helen's children was to read the "Who Am I's" and, drawing on the knowledge contained in the letters they had received, try to match them with the photos and the name labels.

Soon after this, a grand meeting of the children was planned in Victory Park, which is situated between the two schools and within walking distance. The Moonee Ponds West children wore name tags and carried the photographs, name labels, and "Who Am I's" with them. When the two groups came together the teachers were introduced and then the children had to find their pen pals.

One kindergarten girl had been informed by letter that her pen pal was a boy, but at the actual meeting, she was in total shock that her pal was indeed a boy! After the initial surprise she played happily with him for the rest of the afternoon. One second-grade boy had drawn for his pen pal a student with Down syndrome. He had not been told beforehand. He played so caringly the whole afternoon with his newfound friend, gently pushing him on the swing. Many parents of the Moonee Ponds West School attended this meeting. They too were interested to meet their children's pen pals.

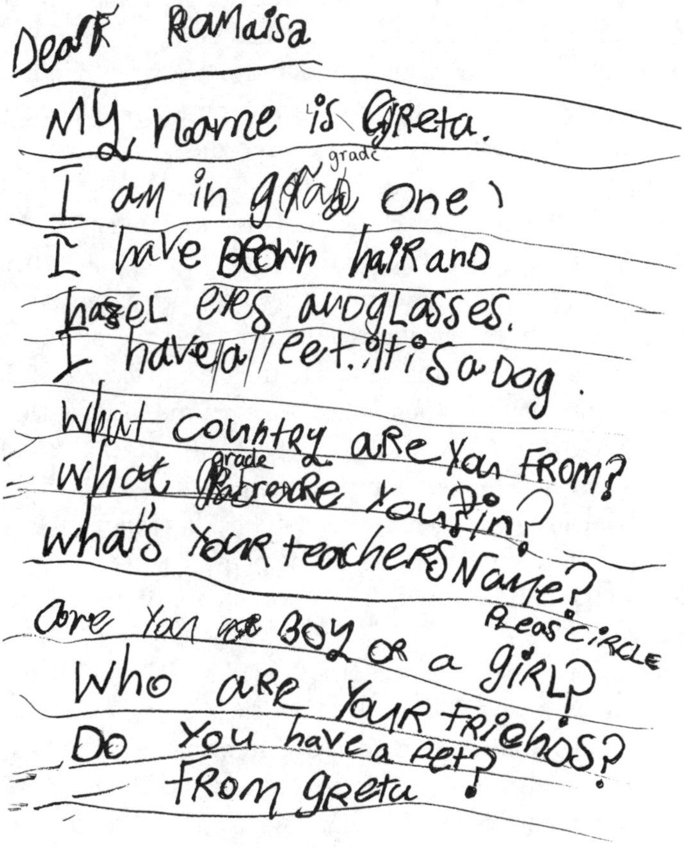

Dear Ramaisa

My name is Greta.
I am in grade One
I have Brown hair and
hazel eyes and glasses.
I have a pet. It is a Dog.

What country are you FROM?
what grade are you in?
what's your teachers Name? Pleas CIRCLE

Are you a BOY or a GIRL?
Who are Your FRIENDS?
Do you have a pet?
FROM greta

Dear Ramaisa
My name is greta.
I am in grade one
I have Brown hair and
hazel eyes and glasses.
I have a pet. It is a Dog.
what country are you from?
what GadraRe you in?
what's your teachers NaMe"
Are you a Boy oR a girl?
Who aRe Your FrienDs?
Do you have a Pet?
FroM greta
Greta

Figure 3–5

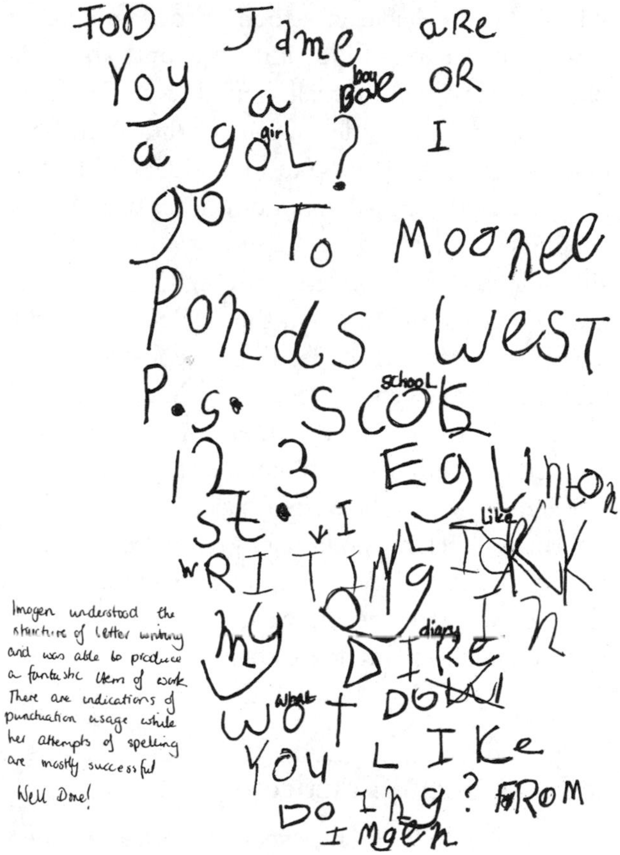

FoD Jame aRe
Yoy a ~~boy~~ Boy OR
a goL? I
go To Moonee
Ponds West
P.s. SCOL [school]
123 Eglinton
ST. I wRITING LIKK [like]
my DIRE [diary] IN
Wot [what] DOb
YOU LIKe
DOIng? FROM
Imgen

Imogen understood the
structure of letter writing
and was able to produce
a fantastic item of work.
There are indications of
punctuation usage while
her attempts of spelling
are mostly successful.

Well Done!

For Jayme, are
a boy or
a girl? I
go to Moonee
Ponds West P.S.
123 Eglinton
St. I like
writing in
my diary
What do
you like
doing? From
Imogen

Figure 3–6

The teachers felt it was one of the best things they had ever organized in their teaching careers. One small first-grade boy told his Ascot Vale West teacher at the end of the day, "It has been the best day of my life."

Back at school in Vicki and Helen's classroom, two class Big Books were compiled and published. One was a collection of individual recounts about the day. The second was compiled in small groups with each small group brainstorming and writing around a subtopic; how we got there; how we felt; what we did. Both books included many photographs taken on the day. It is now up to individual children to continue writing to their pen pals if they so desire. Email communication will also be possible through their classroom computers.

Interestingly, the children have reported many sightings of their pals at local facilities such as the Ascot Vale Leisure Centre and the Auskick Competition (an Australian Rules football-kicking competition). It is hoped these friendships will continue within the local community. This endeavor, which engaged the children in writing authentically, has helped them get to know and befriend others in their community, some of whom are from different economic and cultural groups. If we hope to teach for a better world, it is important for young children to meet others from backgrounds unlike their own, to play with them, to enjoy them—all before community prejudices set in.

Pen-pal programs between children from different schools are not new. What was impressive in this instance was that the end was not writing; the end was for children to apply rights and responsibilities familiar to them in the school situations to a social situation outside their school.

Summary: Literacy as Social Practice

Today, language including literacy is seen as social practice. All the world's people listen, speak, read, and write for purposes necessary for participation in life activities. There is no useful end in writing for writing's sake. No one reads writing that does not serve some meaningful purpose. Today, with new technologies, we are able to write or create texts that challenge traditional ideas of what it is to be literate. Many young people are literate in ways older generations are not. To captivate students by the possibilities of literacy in their lives, schools must ensure that the literacy practices of the school curriculum are seen by the students to be relevant. If students are to be empowered by literacy and confident in their abilities to read and write and express their opinions in the wider community, they must see some match between how they read and write in school time with how they read and write out of school.

References

Carrington, V. 2001. "Emergent Home Literacies: A Challenge for Educators." *The Australian Journal of Language and Literacy*, 24(2).

Cambourne, B. 1988. *The Whole Story: Natural Learning and the Acquisition of Literacy in the Classroom*. Auckland, New Zeland: Ashton Scholastic.

Gee, J. 1990. *Social Linguistics and Literacies: Ideology in Discourses*. London: Falmer Press.

Smith, F. 1984. "The Creative Achievement of Literacy." In *Awakening to Literacy*, edited by H. Goelman and A. Oberg. London: Heinemann Educational Books.

WAN2TLK? Ltle bk of txt msgs. 2000. London: Michael O'Mara Books Ltd.

CHAPTER 4

TEXT TYPES AND GENRES

Language is social practice: language is an integral part of life activities. As the activity changes, so does the accompanying language. Think for a moment about the language of sailors competing in an ocean yacht race. Now compare this to the language of a parent-teacher interview. These are different social occasions and, thus, the language is different. Not only does the language differ but also what the participants do, how they behave, and what they wear (Gee 1990). The language of different life activities or social practices develops with the activities; the language is part and parcel of the practice, be it scoring a tennis match or addressing a conference of one's colleagues. The language facilitates satisfactory engagement in the activity.

Classification of Language Uses (Tough)

The inherent understanding that language is social practice, that different social practices demand different language use means that we, as teachers, must be familiar with a respected classification of language uses, for only then can we evaluate our teaching programs and the breadth of language use or purposes to which we are exposing children. In some classrooms there is an imbalance of language purposes, with children asked to recount or report on class activities for a large proportion of their written work.

Joan Tough (1977) identified the following language use in the oral language of young children:

> self-maintaining (e.g., referring to physical and psychological needs)
>
> directing (e.g., directing the actions of self and others)
>
> reporting on present and past experiences (e.g., labelling components of scene; making comparisons)
>
> toward logical reasoning (e.g., recognizing causal and dependent relationships; drawing conclusions)
>
> predicting (e.g., anticipating and forecasting events)
>
> projecting (e.g., projecting into the experiences and feelings of others)

Imagining (e.g., developing an imaginary situation based on real life or on fantasy). (Tough 1977, 23)

Writing to Project

Tough described projecting as empathizing with the experiences, the feelings, and the reactions of others and to situations never experienced. All of the above language purposes are part and parcel of everyday life, but if we are to develop students with the capacity to think and feel as others and to work toward social justice, the language of projecting is particularly important.

Each year at Moonee Ponds West Primary School a Fun Run is held with all children participating. The purpose of the Fun Run is to raise money for some deserving cause. It is the members of the Junior School Council who choose the charity to which the funds raised are given. In other words the children, not the teachers, determine where the money goes. (JSC is the children's governing body, consisting of representatives voted for from the children in each grade in the school. The JSC is another way of involving children in democracy.) This year JSC determined that the funds would be given to the Lions Club International Mobility Centre for the purchase of Hart Walkers to help children with cerebral palsy to walk. Each year at the Fun Run, children solicit friends and family members to sponsor them. Sponsors pay a small amount for each circle of the school block completed by a child. Parents assist throughout the day acting as marshals and first-aid attendants. Prior to the actual event this year, Jan Hayes, the phys. ed. teacher, borrowed a video about the Hart Walker for the children to view. Footage showed a cerebral palsied child's elation on taking a few first steps using the walker. When the video finished there was no class discussion. The teachers asked each child to write about "What's on your mind after watching the video." This writing prompt is open-ended. It allows children to write however they wish—to recount a related personal experience or to express an opinion or to write analytically.

Lions Club International Mobility Centre

What a great charity to raise money for. We do the Fun Run and walk a few kilometres when those kids just want to walk a few steps. Just because 300 kids can't walk is why we should raise as much money as we can. The Lions International Mobility Centre is doing a great thing by giving kids options for the ability to walk.

Imagine being a parent, thinking your child can't walk but then all of a sudden a group of people come along offering the chance for your child to walk. It would be like a miracle.

I never knew how lucky I was to play footy tennis and many other sports when children with cerebral palsy can't even walk.

For all these reasons I say we sponsor the Lions International Mobility Centre for every Fun Run and Jump Rope for Heart, not only this year but for many years to come.

—Chris, grade 6

In Chris' writing, note in paragraph one how he projects into the children's intentions: ". . . those kids just want to walk a few steps." In paragraph two he projects in to the feelings of the parents. "Imagine being a parent, thinking your child can't walk but then all of a sudden a group of people come along, offering the chance for your child to walk. It would be like a miracle."

To See Happy Smiles

I did not do the Fun Run for fun. I did it to help those kids with cerebral palsy. I felt sad when I saw the video because those kids could not walk or run and I would hate not to walk or run.

It would be so hard because you would not be able to play soccer or tiggy. I felt sad when I saw the smiles on the kids' faces when they took one step. I would smile too when I took my first step.

It is good the Lions Club helped David Hart to bring the Hart Walker in to Australia.

I want to see as many kids in a walking frame as possible.

I ran as hard as I could to help those kids.

It costs a lot of money for a Hart Walker, so our Fun Run was to help kids with cerebral palsy.

I hope we raised a lot of money because the Hart Walker cost so much-$5,000. Wouldn't it be great if a big company sponsored the manufacture of the Hart Walker then we could see a lot more smiles on those faces.

—MICHAEL, GRADE 5

Michael, too, projects in his response. "It would be so hard because you would not be able to play soccer or tiggy." Michael also predicts how it would be if some company sponsored the manufacture of the walkers.

If we want to work for a more just society, then we need knowledge about all forms of disadvantage. We need knowledge of those for whom life is difficult. We need knowledge about taxes and the distribution of public monies. Primary school is not too soon to introduce studies in classrooms about those who are different—physically or mentally or culturally or economically—from the mainstream group. The issue should not be one of charity for the disadvantaged, of those with money choosing to give to those who do not, but a recognition that we are all human, that we are responsible for one another. Otherwise, how do we ensure a more equitable distribution of the world's wealth so more people can be financially independent and not have to rely on handouts from others?

Classification of Language Uses (Smith)

Frank Smith, adapting the work of Halliday (1973), developed the following classification of language uses. It is not limited to the language of young children.

1. Instrumental: getting things done; satisfying material needs
2. Regulatory: controlling the behavior and feelings of others

3. Interactional: establishing relationships and relative status with others
4. Personal: expressing individuality, awareness of self, feelings
5. Heuristic: seeking and testing new knowledge
6. Imaginative: creating new worlds; making up stories, poems
7. Representational: communicating information
8. Divertive: creating puns, jokes, riddles
9. Authoritative/contractual: describing statutes, laws, regulations, agreements, contracts
10. Perpetuating: maintaining records, histories, diaries, notes, scores (Smith 1982, 14)

Planning for a Range of Language Uses in Classrooms

Smith (1982) in his classification of language uses includes interactional language, the language of "me and you" or getting along with others, and the language of "me against you" establishing separateness. If we hope to have children behaving in socially competent ways it is indeed important that they know how to use language to interact with others, to establish relationships, to make friends. If children are put down at home, they may not know how to speak kindly to others or how to initiate conversations that build friendships. All children need to be able to use language to form friendships—to know how to speak to gain entry into other children's activities without causing resentment.

Also from Smith's list is divertive language or the language of having fun, of making people laugh. Life is very serious for many children today. There must be some time in their day when they can laugh. Not only students but teachers too need authentic reasons to laugh at school.

When evaluating their class language programs, teachers must ensure that the language of social interaction and humor is not neglected. A well-rounded teaching program has children using language for all of Smith's language purposes as illustrated in Table 4.

Functional Grammar

In the late 1980s the work of the 1970s around language purposes was further developed by the genrists, who described the relationship between text purpose and text shape. Their work was responsible for what became known as functional grammar.

According to the genrists, the context of any language event can be described according to field, tenor, and mode (Collerson 1994). The *field* describes the human activity being engaged in: sports, medicine, shopping, the stock market. The *tenor* described the relationship between the people taking part: employer/employee, teacher/

Table 4   Possible Written Texts to Achieve a Range of Language Purposes and Uses

Language Purposes (Tough 1977)	Written Texts
Self-Maintaining	Signs for construction or building: "Do not touch"
	Labelling, books, lockers, clothes
	Justifying behavior
Directing	Instructions to play a board game
	Directions for a treasure hunt
	Meeting agenda
	School concert program
	Procedure for making some toy
	Directions to a child's home
Reporting on Present and Past Experiences	Recounts
	Reports for the class magazine
	A news report for the school radio (speaker system)
	Letters telling of things done
	Writing a summary of something read
	Making comparisons about two films or two books or two excursions
	Writing an information report
Toward Logical Reasoning	Writing an explanation of how something was made or done
	Writing to explain how something works
	Letter arguing for some cause
	Article for the school magazine arguing the case for something
	Writing to justify some action
	Writing the case for some new classroom equipment
	Writing for a particular consequence as a result of transgressing an agreed class responsibility

continues

Table 4 *(Continued)*

Language Purposes (Tough 1977)	Written Texts
Predicting	Writing a prediction before completing a science experiment
	Predicting what will happen next in a story
	Predicting what children will see on an excursion, e.g., which animals will be at the zoo
	Predicting the effects of some natural phenomenon
Projecting	Writing in role as a book character
	Describing a character's feelings in a narrative
	Writing to someone who has suffered misfortune
	Written conversations in a role
	Poem describing what some event may have been like for participants
Imagining	Writing an imaginative story developed while using dress-up clothes
	Writing an imaginative story that begins with some real event
	Writing an original imaginative story
	Writing a poem of an imagined event
	Writing a fictional play

Language Uses (Smith 1982)	Written Texts
Instrumental: I want	(see Self-Maintaining, above)
Regulatory: Do as I tell you	(see Directing, above)
Interactional: Me and you	Writing letters of welcome to new students; letters of congratulation
	Writing letters with good wishes on birthdays and seasonal celebrations
	Writing invitations
	Writing dialogue for story characters
	Written conversations
	Using language in small-group discussions so everyone is included

continues

Table 4 (*Continued*)

Language Uses (Smith 1982)	Written Texts
Personal: Here I come	Writing personally of feelings; sorrow, pride, anger, contentment Writing a time line of your own life Writing of team loyalties, hobbies Poems about self A personal literature response Self-evaluation of progress at school
Heuristic: Tell me why?	Heuristic: Tell me why Planning surveys, science experiments Writing letters seeking information Writing questions for visiting speakers Asking questions of literature Posing and testing hypotheses in scientific and social investigations
Imaginative: Let's pretend	(see Imagining, above)
Representational: I've got something to tell you	(see Reporting, above)
Divertive: Enjoy this	Writing innovation on published rhyme or story, with the students as characters, to have some fun Write an unexpected ending for traditional tale Write humorous story, rhyme, or poem Write play that is a comedy, e.g., fractured fairytales Rewrite well-known tale from another perspective. An example of this is *The True Story of the Three Little Pigs* (Scieszka 1996)
Authoritative/contractual: How it must be	Children participate in forming class rights, responsibilities, and consequences Children participate in formulating agreed rules and consequences for school ground Children invent board games and list rules of play In writing fiction, children include rules for some club membership Agreed class deadlines for completion of work
Perpetuating: How it was	Diaries Time lines Historical recount

student, doctor/patient. The *mode* describes the type of language being used: spoken or written, conversation between two people, an address to a large audience, a written essay. The relationship between text purpose and language use (text shape and linguistic items) is thus more readily elaborated when one understands the context for the language use in terms of field, tenor, and mode. A conversation between two people (mode), about child care (field), differs if the relationship (tenor) changes. For example, two inexperienced parents chatting on this topic would be using language differently than would two child-care professionals.

Besides the immediate context for the language event as described by field, tenor, and mode, the genrists also pointed out the impact of the broader, cultural context. Think of the language differences between speakers of North American English and speakers of Australian English. Not only do the accents differ, but also vocabulary items and local idioms.

Nonfiction Genre

The genrists argued that for students to access the worlds of tertiary education and business they needed competence in the nonfiction texts of those domains, especially the genres of argument, information report, description, procedure, and explanation. There are other nonfiction genres—for example, biography, but the genrists highlighted these few as being necessary for all students, particularly disadvantaged students, if they were to gain social advancement and entry into the world of business and higher education.

From the understanding of the contextual settings for language purposes came an understanding of the relationship between text purpose, text shape, and linguistic items. "Depending on the purpose of a text, it will have a particular text shape or schematic structure, and it will have specific linguistic features that we can identify and describe" (Hammond 1988, 26).

Leaving aside nonfiction texts for a moment, let us consider the purpose and structure of a narrative, whose main purpose is to entertain the reader. While it is true that some narratives teach about other times or other places, in general the overriding purpose for reading narrative is to be entertained.

QUESTION: Do you prefer writing fiction or nonfiction?
JACQUI (AGE FOURTEEN): Fiction. It's a lot freer. I like to have the options. When I writing a story it takes me with it—I don't plan it out beforehand. I think of the start then as I write I go back and change something, so the plot can keep moving.

The structure of most narratives evolves from following a character or characters, in a series of events, throughout a story. We are introduced to the main character in the initial *orientation*, and follow him as he meets and is involved in some *complication*(s), and works through to some *resolution*. Complications hook us in and keep us reading. In order to engage us with the character, the events of the story are laid out in a sequential form. That is, we read narrative in a linear way, from front to back. The narrative is constructed around individual characters, or what the genrists call *specific participants*. The telling of the story involves all verb types or processes, action (*dig*), mental (*think*), and talking (*yell*).

In contrast, genrists would label a book about sharks, for example, the information report. The purpose of an information report differs from that of a narrative. Its purpose is to convey factual information about a class of things. The information about sharks is grouped around subtopics, which become the chapter headings; for instance, breeding habits, life cycles, or great white sharks. Rather than having a linear structure, which requires reading from start to finish, this text has a table of contents to assist readers in retrieving information and finding their particular starting points. The table of contents lists the chapters or subtopics, thus enabling the reader to turn to the chapter containing the information he needs. There is no plot to be engaged with, no sequence of events to follow, so one does not have to observe a linear route through the book. In fact, one does not have to read the whole book. There are no individual characters. The participants in this text are not specific but general—sharks, predators, blue pointers. Because the book is factual, no personal pronouns are used. Personal opinion is not part of this text. The language is factual and precise, with many action verbs, (*eat, attack, swim*). Because the text is conveying information about how a class of things is, or exists, it is generally written in the timeless present tense (*are, have*) There are no characters to engage in conversation so there are no talking verbs (*said, replied, whispered*).

Nonfiction Genres: Text Purpose, Text Shape or Structure, and Linguistic Items

Table 5 on pages 68 and 69 lists the nonfiction genres that the genrists felt were essential components of study in the primary-school writing program. Included with each are the main organizing features and the specific language items. Note how it is the function or purpose of the text that determines both the overall structure and which linguistic items are appropriate.

Genre and Process Writing

Somewhat unfortunately coinciding with the introduction of the nonfiction genre to the writing curriculum, attacks were made on what was commonly known as Process Writing and on the work of Donald Graves. In the early 1980s very little factual writing was done in classrooms by students. It was thought then that factual writing was the province of high schools. In process classrooms where children had choice over what they wrote, they obviously wrote in forms with which they were familiar—basically, recount and narrative. How could they write in genres they had never experienced, either by reading independently or by being read to?

Today, largely as a result of the genrists influence, there are many books written in the nonfiction genre that are very suitable for use in primary classrooms. Teachers read aloud these texts and students read them individually as part of class studies. When students are immersed in a genre and see demonstrations of how this genre is written, they approximate it in their own attempts and, with further experience, they refine their understandings and writing of the genre.

Sadly, with the attacks on the work of Graves, much of the process-writing work ceased; however, it should be an integral part of any writing classroom. All writing involves a *process*. You cannot write without engaging in a process. Do you research beforehand? Do you write one quick draft or many? Do you publish the writing? Holistic classrooms include writing and reading in many genres, including those outlined above, as well as in the genres of everyday texts (magazines, posters, cartoons). Children in these classrooms engage with the writing process as they compose the nonfiction genre relevant to the studies they are undertaking.

The Decontextualized Teaching of Genre

An unfortunate by-product of the work of the genrists has been decontextualized instruction of the particular genres. Rather than teaching a genre because it was necessary to complete some area of study in the curriculum, the genre became the goal. The teaching was separated from the social practice of which it was an integral component. Lists of structures hung in classrooms and myriad children were directed to observe these when constructing a text with no consideration given to the context and purpose for constructing that text. As Lucy Calkins said, "many researchers argue that knowing the characteristics of ideal finished products has little to do with developing the skills to produce those products. Students may be able to recite the characteristics of a tall tale, but his does not mean they can write one" (1986, 14).

In the field of language education, the genrists contributed much about the nature of texts and the relationship between text shape and text purpose. However, their work did not advocate the decontextualized, direct instruction method for teaching genre. "A functional approach to language does not advocate teaching about language by handing down prescriptive recipes. Rather it is concerned with providing information about the development of effective texts for particular purposes, and providing it at the point of need within the context of real purposeful language use" (Derewianka 1990, 5).

Some state writing curriculum documents have been consumed by the nonfiction genre. Hierarchies have been developed that specify which nonfiction genres are taught and at which grade level. These hierarchies have no foundation in research. What is significant in a child's coming to write with competence in one of these genres is whether he has read examples of this text type, or had them read to him; whether he has taken part in class constructions of the genre; whether he and his classmates have discussed the structure and linguistic items in the context of using the genre; and most importantly, whether there has been authentic purpose for him to write in this genre. Let me say again: I agree that nonfiction texts should be part of the primary school curriculum.

Table 5   Suggested Essential Nonfiction Genres

Genre	Purpose	Structure	Linguistic Items
Recount	To record something that happened in the past; may be personal or factual about others	Orientation Sequence of events as they unfolded sometime in the past Personal opinion/comment may be included	Specific participants Past-tense action verbs; if personal recount it may have mental and talking verbs. May include personal opinions and feelings Factual recount about others: precise details included, third-person pronouns Words depicting sequence: *next, before, then*
Information Report	To provide factual information about a class of things	Table of contents May begin with a general statement about the species or phenomena being described Information is grouped around subtopics May, but not always, end with a general statement May include index and glossary Visuals are important to support and supplement the information provided; e.g., labelled diagrams, graphs, photos, maps	No specific characters but rather, generalized participants (*kangaroos, wallabies, joeys*) Descriptive, factual language Some action verbs (*hop, destroy, eat*) Written in the present (*is, are, have*) Language to compare and classify (*are like, unlike, taller, smaller*) Objective writing style; personal opinions are not appropriate
Procedure	To outline how to complete something; e.g., how to make a cake, how to play a game, how to build a dining-room table	Aim/goal (usually written as the heading) Equipment needed Procedure to follow Numbers and diagrams may be part of the text	Generalized participants (*players, cards*) Action verbs (*deal, cut, draw*) Words indicating time (*then, after, next*) Audience is general (*You deal; You chop*) Precise factual details (*a small teaspoon; cook until starting to bubble*)

	Purpose	Structure	Language Features
Argument	To argue for or against an issue	Introduction of the issue with the position taken by the writer List of reasons for the position taken; should be discussion of and supporting evidence for the reasons included Conclusion with reaffirmation of writer's position	Participants may be individual persons or events but more often they are generalized (*old-growth forests*) Variety of verb types, including mental (*think, believe*) Connecting words to do with reasoning (*so, because, therefore*) Passive case may be used Nominalization may be used to bring a more objective voice (The *destruction* of the old. . . .) Because this is a personal view, argument may contain some emotive words (We *adamantly believe*; we protest in the *strongest* terms; we *passionately* . . .)
Explanation	To explain how something works or why something is as it is	Statement about the matter being explained, which is sometimes written as a question (How do the lungs work?) Explanation of process	Generalized participants Timeless present tense (*exist, are, have*) Time relationships (*first, next, after*) Cause-and-effect relationships (*so, because*) Mainly action verbs (*rises, falls*)

They are used and learned in the context of class and personal investigations. But if we are only educating children to write for work and higher education we are neglecting important purposes for education; we are neglecting important dimensions of human existence. What about the wider view of the world and the world's people? What about the texts important in the children's lives? What about the capacity to learn about ourselves and others? What about the capacity to empathize and feel for others? What about the language of wondering? What about laughing and having fun? To refer to classifications of language purposes such as those of Smith (1982) and Tough (1977) helps broaden our perception of what is possible in classroom language programs and what is possible in children's lives.

Genre and Flexibility

The genrists use of the term *genre* differs from previous understandings of the word, as in *literary* genre—poems, plays, and quality stories. Poems got scant mention from the genrists because a poem may serve a whole range of purposes; a poem may be a story or a description or a recount or the expression of a feeling. Those genres identified by the genrists each served a quite specific purpose. Many language educators and professional writers argue that in the real world there is considerable flexibility in adapting genre to other purposes, and in constructing new ways of achieving particular writing purposes. Not all narratives follow the schematic structure of orientation, complication, and resolution. Many narratives have more than one problem. Sometimes the story begins with the problem.

Some of the most ingenious, successful books are those that break traditional understandings of what is expected. An example is the Magic School Bus series by Joanne Cole. This author has written what appear at first glance to be picture storybooks. The central character is a rather wonderful teacher called Ms. Frizzle, who has some amazing powers, particularly when in charge of the school bus. She can take all her students anywhere she wants to go in this bus. For example, during a class study of water, she takes them to the top of a cloud where they get out of the bus and change into raindrops. What is different about these books is that they combine a fantasy narrative with important factual information around the edges of the pages.

I notice that teachers do not use these books as picture storybooks; by that I mean the books are not used at quiet story time. Rather, they are used as resource books in class studies. *The Magic School Bus at the Waterworks* is used as a factual information resource during a class study of water.

Personal and Required Classroom Writing

A class writing program is made up of both personal writing and required writing. In the required strand new genres or text types are introduced and demonstrated, all as part of some authentic need related to class interests and investigations. Children are required to write in these genres. Their first attempts may be approximations, but with further immersions and demonstrations the student writing moves closer to the required conventional form.

In the personal strand, the child chooses whatever she wishes to write about and in which form, and whether the writing goes to publication. But whether the child is writing according to her choice or as required by the teacher, she engages in a writing process. In evaluating the purposes for which children write in the class program, the class teacher's perspective should be guided by some classifications of language use, such as those of Smith (1982) and Tough (1977), to ensure that the children experience a wide variety of purposes, including personal, interpersonal, and public (see Table 6).

Table 6 Possible Authentic Contexts for Using and Learning About Nonfiction Genres

Nonfiction Genre	Context (learning about)
Information Report	Sea Creatures Machines Butterflies
Procedure	Food: recipes Games: instructions for playing The Human Body: how to do CPR
Argument	The Environment: It is okay to log old-growth forests; Private motor vehicles should be banned from the central city. Water: The watering of lawns should be banned during daylight hours. School Issues: The schoolyard should be available for use by all students, not just the older boys with their footballs.
Explanation	The Human Body: How the lungs work. How the heart works. Why exercise is good for the human body. Our planet: Why we have night and day.

Classroom Practice

Be Explicit About the Purposes for Writing

When constructing a class text, always explain why it is being done. If the children are jointly making a factual book about the butterflies they have been studying, talk with them about why they are writing it. What is their purpose in making the book? What will the book contain? Who might their audience be?

Writing to Project

If education is to develop students who have the capacity to work for world peace and social justice for all, they must be able to think and feel as others. The following are some activities that promote empathy:

- When reading narratives require students to speak as one of the characters at a particular point in the story; describe what a character might be feeling at a poignant point in the story; and rewrite the story (or one scene) from the point of view of one of the characters.
- Have children write as someone who has been teased or bullied at school; someone who is new to the school.
- Have children speak or write as someone featured in the news.

Plan for Learning About a Genre While Using the Genre

When planning an integrated unit of study or inquiry, explore the print resources necessary for the study. If procedural texts will be important to the inquiry work, plan for the children to simultaneously learn about the structure of these texts. Alternately, if, as part of the study, the children will be reading from the information report genre, plan to simultaneously study the construction of these texts.

Construct Charts Comparing Different Genres

When studying a particular genre have the children compare it with a more familiar genre. For instance, younger children are generally most familiar with storybooks or narrative. Place piles of both storybooks and information report texts on clusters of tables or on the carpet. In small groups the children sort the books into two piles: storybooks and information books. Then the children explain how they knew which were the information books and which were the storybooks while someone records their responses on a chart.

Kindergarten and first-grade children generally identify the following features:

Storybooks	Information Reports
not true	true
different drawings	has factual information
has different titles	has real photos
about different things, like	has table of contents
witches and dragons	has labelled diagrams

This is just knowledge the children have at the start of the study, but it lets the teacher know which text features to focus on in the weeks ahead; for example:

Where can we start reading this information book?

Where do we begin reading a storybook?

How do we find the information we are looking for? (Use the table of contents or the index.)

How is the index different from the table of contents?

Who is the storybook about?

Who is the main character?

Are there individual characters in these books about sharks?

In the storybooks, the characters talk to one another. How do we know in the text where the characters are talking? (Quotation marks)

Do characters speak in information texts?

Do we see speech in quotation marks in information texts?

Students from grade 4–6 could work in small groups to compare two genres they have studied as part of integrated studies.

Information Texts	Procedural Texts
gives information about a group of things	tells you how to do something
uses full sentences, longer sentences	lists things you need
doesn't use "I" or "me"	the method sometimes has dot points
descriptive language	shorter language
table of contents	words that tell you what to do,
index	like, *put, stir, heat*
glossary	you need to follow the order of the text
you can start reading anywhere	

Use Bundling in the Construction of Class Information Reports

As part of a study of frogs, information reports could be an accompanying language study. After reading and looking at many of these texts the teacher and children could jointly write a book about frogs, sharing all they have learned. The process might look something like this:

• Each child writes a statement about frogs on a large piece of paper, using a felt pen. (The writing needs to be big enough to be read by classmates sitting in a circle.)

- The children sit in a whole-class circle and listen as individuals read aloud their statements. For each statement, classmates listen to check that the statement is true; and that it sounds like book language. Whenever a statement is challenged the challenger and writer leave the circle and edit the statement together.
- When all the statements have been checked for accuracy and for book language, they are scattered in the center of the class circle. Individual children are asked to find statements that belong together. The teacher explains how they are preparing the text for the chapters by grouping the statements around subtopics.
- The children form small groups of four to five. Each group is given a bundle of statements that have been formed around a subtopic. The children spread out the statements and sequence them in the best possible order. Each group then reads their sequence to the class. The class considers whether there is important information yet to be included. If so, volunteers write the necessary statements. If the sequence is accepted, the statement strips are numbered, 1, 2, 3, and so on.
- The class helps name each section of the book.
- The section names are each written on a piece of paper and scattered in the middle of the class circle. Different children create a proposed sequence for the sections, which will become the table of contents.
- The children then determine important publishing decisions, such as print style, art medium, and landscape or portrait shape.

Learning to Write in the Genre of Argument

For teachers interested in working for social justice, argument is an important genre to include in the primary school program, for argument can be a genre of action. Because of the lack of models in this genre suited to primary-school-aged students, it is imperative that the teacher demonstrate, both orally and in writing, the language of argument. I outline a sequence of sessions designed to teach upper-primary-school students to write well-constructed arguments.

- Introduce the issue for discussion; for instance, "In the interest of improving air quality, all access to the central business district of our city by car should be denied." The issue may arise from a topic of study or may be suggested by the students. Remember, competence and control in writing a particular genre comes when it is used for some authentic purpose. In upper primary school classrooms, you can display a list of issues, to which children add items they feel are worthy of argument. These issues often relate to observance of particular school routines.
- Students work in pairs, with one the reporter and one the recorder, for fifteen to twenty minutes, listing as many reasons for and against the issue as they can. I have found it is good mental exercise for children to list arguments for each side of an issue, not just those that support their particular opinion. Identifying reasons for the alternate perspective helps students formulate their own argument in defense of their position.

- Students sit in a whole-class circle for sharing and discussion. The chairperson opens the discussion saying something like: "I am the chairperson. My role is to invite reporters to report. I will then invite members from the whole group to speak in support of or against the given argument. My role is to encourage everyone to contribute and to ensure that the discussion is not dominated by one or two people." This role should be introduced and modelled by the teacher for approximately three sessions. Then, in subsequent sessions, a volunteer student can chair the discussion.

     In the very early sessions, if children are not familiar with the language of argument, the teacher will need to make contributions such as, "I would like to support the reasoning of . . ." or "I disagree quite strongly with the point made by the last speaker for the following reason . . ."

- The first sessions involve the students in oral work only, where they learn to use the language of debate and argument. At the end of these sessions the teacher might demonstrate writing her own position on the particular issue. As she writes, she talks explicitly about the structure of written argument: "I begin by writing the issue. Now I list the reasons for believing as I do. To conclude or finish off I will state my position or what I believe on the issue."

- Generally, the students are ready to begin writing by the fourth session. It is a good idea in the first writing session to let the children work in pairs to list some reasons for and against the issue, but when it comes to writing the argument, all children should write their particular opinions individually. As the children write, so does the teacher. At the class share time, the teacher shares her writing and teaches to needs revealed in the children's attempts.

Everyday Texts and Genres

It is important for teachers to teach and incorporate a wide range of text types in classroom studies, including everyday texts. For example, if a child brings an announcement to class from a local newspaper about the birth of a new brother or sister, and then other children bring birth notices of their new siblings, a class discussion could occur around the similarities of each announcement. For example, What does each birth announcement contain?

names of parents (or grandparents)
date of birth
name and sex of baby
place birth occurred
weight (optional)

Children might try to write their own birth announcements. It is important that class writing programs include varied everyday texts as well as the nonfiction genre and the more traditional literary genre such as poems and plays.

Summary: Different Language Purposes, Text Types, and Genres

What is appropriate language in any situation is determined by the purpose, field, tenor, and mode. School language curriculum must build confidence in using language for a host of different purposes. While competence in the nonfiction genre helps students gain access to the business and tertiary education arenas, proactively working for a better world requires other language purposes, especially the capacity to project into the thoughts and feelings of others—to empathize. Important too, is the inclusion of text types that reflect students' lives if they are to see the writing curriculum as having relevance for them.

References

Calkins, L. 1986. *The Art of Teaching Writing*, Portsmouth, NH: Heinemann.

Collerson, J. 1994. *English Grammar: A Functional Approach*. Newtown, New South Wales: Primary English Teaching Association,

Derewianka, B. 1990. *Exploring How Texts Work*. Newtown, New South Wales: Primary English Teaching Association.

Gee, J. 1990. *Social Linguistics and Literacies: Ideology in Discourses*. London: Falmer Press.

Graves, D. 1983. *Teachers and Children at Work*. Portsmouth NH: Heinemann.

Halliday, M. 1973. *Explorations in the Functions of Language*. London: Arnold.

Hammond, J. 1988. "Read Me Your Story . . ." In *Writing for Life*, edited by J. Collerson. Newtown, New South Wales: Primary English Teaching Association.

Smith, F. 1982. *Writing and the Writer*. London: Heinemann Educational Books.

Tough, J. 1977. *Talking and Learning*. London: Ward Lock Educational.

Children's Books
Cole, J. 1986. *The Magic School Bus at the Waterworks*. New York: Scholastic.

Scieszka, J. 1996. *The True Story of the Three Little Pigs*. New York: Penguin.

CHAPTER 5

LEARNING LANGUAGE AS WE LEARN THE WORLD

The predominant view of writing in our society is that it is a tool for communication, for transmission of information. But writing is also a way of "coming to know"—a way of organising out thoughts, of figuring things out, of making meaning of our experiences and "fragile thoughts."

—JEFFREY N. GOLUB (2003, 7)

An early view of learning saw children as empty receptacles. It was the teacher's job to pour discrete pieces of information into the learners. Something need only be taught once. This was the top-off-the-tank or bank-deposit theory of learning. Today, rather than being passive with the teacher doing all the work, the learner is seen as being active in the learning process. Learning is about making new understandings. But what does this mean? In making new understandings, or learning, the learner takes in new information, assesses it against old information, and then maybe rejects this information or, alternatively, blends it with preexisting knowledge, thereupon forming new understandings or making adjustments to previous knowledge.

As we experience the world directly, and as we listen and read, we meet new ideas, new ways of seeing the world. As we speak or write about these ideas, we make greater sense of them. As we talk or write we tease out concepts; we ponder, we hypothesize, we imagine, and so come to understand in our own particular ways. Think for a moment of a film you have seen recently. Were you left with puzzles? Were you able to talk through these puzzles with someone else who saw the film? Were your interpretations clarified? I recently saw *Confessions of a Dangerous Mind*, and for the last ten days I have been asking friends if they have seen this same film. I desperately need to talk about it. I don't quite understand . . . was it real or fantasy? If it was real, how can the supposed CIA agent write about it? I need to talk to someone to achieve a better understanding of this film.

Similarly, the act of writing provides the opportunity to confront and sharpen cloudy understandings, to pose and detail solutions to problems, to formulate and develop creative ideas. Of course such writing is not one-draft writing. It is writing that takes time and occurs in fits and starts as ideas are born. Space between writing episodes is often necessary for the safe nurturing and development of these ideas. However, as Stephen Krashen remarked, "School teaches us the opposite. School teaches us that we write to display what we already know, not to discover new ideas" (2003, 77).

We learn by listening, talking, reading, and writing. Language is integral to the learning process. Emmitt, Pollock, and Komesaroff break down the language/learning process in the following way:

- acquiring/generating knowledge
- processing/making connections
- drawing conclusions/hypothesizing
- consolidating and applying knowledge/evaluating one's learning (2003, 224)

When we understand the role of language in learning we appreciate that language cannot be an isolated study in the school curriculum. As children talk and write and listen and read to make understandings in every curriculum area, they are simultaneously becoming skillful listeners, speakers, readers, and writers—and they are learning about language.

The Choice Is Yours: Drugs in the Classroom

To illustrate how children simultaneously learn language and learn about language as they use language to learn, I now describe an integrated study unit about drugs, undertaken by Shirl Ramage, Annie Drennan, and their fifty-six grade 5–6 children. This topic was actually initiated after the teachers attended a drug education program, but observing the class activities and reading the children's work on display left no doubt about how child-centered the program was and how much the children learned. The study lasted one term. While I cannot possibly describe everything that happened, I hope to illustrate, using Smith's (1982) classification of language use (see Chapter 4), the variety of language purposes with which the children engaged as they investigated issues within the study.

Tapping Existing Knowledge

In small, cooperative groups, the children listed what they knew about drugs. Much cooperative group work occurs in this double-teaching unit, and the children are familiar with ways of using language to facilitate group work. It is not uncommon to hear utterances like "I like that idea." "What do you think, Michael?" "Let's give Anna a turn." "Does everyone agree with that?" Children working in small groups learn to use language for social interaction, which facilitates working toward a common goal or completion of a common task (Interactional).

Sometimes a child was reminded to wait his turn: "Chris, let Phoebe finish" (Regulatory). Much of the language was used for communicating information or existing knowledge (Representational). Some of the statements were:

Drug makers can put things in their drugs to make it less costly for themselves.

In the Olympics athletes are tested for drugs.

Some people are addicted to sniffing paint—when you sniff from a bag it's called "huffing."

If you have 0.05 in your blood you cannot drive.

Needles can be found on beaches.

Some public toilets have blue lights so that people cannot see their veins if they want to inject.

Lots of drugs have bad side effects.

Cigarettes are bad.

Some people rob and steal to get drugs.

Some marijuana plants don't have a drug effect.

Tapping Existing Knowledge: List Drugs You Know

Individually, children listed the drugs they knew and from this compiled a master list. Some children were obviously acquiring new vocabulary and new knowledge (Representational; Heuristic).

Acquiring New Knowledge: Defining a Drug

The class discussed exactly what a "definition" is, then the children each wrote a definition of a drug:

Drugs are life savers and life takers. They are blood stimulating. Pills, liquids, powders, dried leaves. They are used in hospitals but also used in alleyways and places like that.

—JORDAN, GRADE 6

A drug is a pill/liquid that can kill people if they take too much.

—MARISSA, GRADE 5

Writing definitions from what they knew involved representational use of language. The children pooled their definitions and wrote a class definition.

Class Drug Definition

A drug is a substance that can affect your body in a bad or a good way. It should be used responsibly. It can come in many forms and be taken into the body in various ways (Heuristic).

The class then compared this with the definition given by the Drug Education organization: "A drug is a chemical substance that alters a person's mood or behavior as a result of changes in the brain." Sharing the children's definitions and discussing the definition from the Drug Education organization involved some children in asking questions and seeking clarification (Heuristic).

Acquiring New Knowledge: Visiting Speakers and Videos

During the unit, speakers attended the classroom from the Poisons Information center and from QUIT, an organization that helps smokers to quit smoking. Several children welcomed and thanked all visitors (Interactional). The children viewed several videos; for example, one on the effects of smoking on the body, and shared some personal experiences (Representational; Heuristic; Personal).

Acquiring New Knowledge: Listing and Ranking Drugs

All the children were given a copy of the master list of drugs from an earlier class activity. Working in pairs, they ranked the drugs from the most harmful to the least harmful, and wrote their reasons. In a preliminary discussion, the class agreed on a procedure for accomplishing the task and formulating their findings (Regulatory). One group listed heroin as the most harmful for the following reason: "Heroin can kill you. The first time you have it you may take too much. Lots of people have died from heroin." Their least harmful choice was mylantin. "Mylantin helps you. Hard to have enough to harm you" (Representative; heuristic; toward logical reasoning [see Tough 1977]).

Acquiring New Knowledge: Positive and Negative Effects of Drugs

Once again, the children formed small groups. Each group was given a drug to research. The specific task for each group was to list the positive and negative effects of the drug being investigated. Children had access to the classroom information from the Drug Education package, pamphlets from the Australian Drug Foundation, and websites from Get Wise for their research (Heuristic).

Processing and Making Connections: Role-Play the Effects of Drugs

The groups rehearsed role-plays illustrating the positive and negative effects of the drugs they investigated and later presented them to the whole class (Representational; Divertive).

Processing and Making Connections: The Language of Argument

The use of argument was one of the language aims for this integrated inquiry. The teachers were hoping one outcome would be that the children would be better able to make informed decisions about the part drugs might play in their lives, if any; they wanted them to have opinions and to be able to reason in support of their views. Several issues were the topic of argument.

If a Drug Is Legal It Must Be OK   Working in small groups the children listed as many arguments as they could, both for and against the issue of legal drug use. Only then could they write their personal opinion on this issue (Representational, Personal, Toward Logical Reasoning).

Drug Education Should Only Be Taught in the Home   This was part of the August yearbook page. (For a full explanation of the use of yearbooks, see page 97.) The children were challenged to try to list three arguments both for and against the issue of drug education before writing their opinion. The teachers helped by demonstrating how to write arguments and describing the components of the structure: introduction of the issue; listing of reasons for supporting or disagreeing with the issue; and a concluding statement. Some discussion took place as well about the linguistic elements that occur in written arguments; for example, personal pronouns such as I, we, me. Is it acceptable to use these when arguing a position? Yes, it is; you are airing a personal opinion and so must use these first-person pronouns. How does it compare to writing a factual report about drugs? Would you find these same pronouns in a factual book about drugs? No. Why not? An information report is meant to portray factual knowledge, not personal opinion. In the context of using language to learn about drugs, children were learning about language itself: here, specifically, about the language of written argument.

Processing and Making Connections: Public Forum Role-Play

Once or twice a year public forums are conducted in this grade 5–6 classroom. They usually take place near the end of an integrated unit of study and the children look forward to them. For this study, six community characters related to the topic were nominated and six students volunteered to role-play these characters. The hypothetical topic for this particular forum was whether the school board should accept the Coca-Cola Company's offer to fund the school camp. The characters to be role-played at the forum were the president of the Coca-Cola Company, the president of the school board, a teacher, a student from the children's Junior School Council, and two parents from the school community. Before beginning to prepare their speeches the children determined that the company president, one parent, and the teacher would speak in support of the offer and that the school council president, one parent, and the student would speak against the offer.

During two sessions the six speakers listed arguments they might put forth and then wrote their speeches. They rehearsed their speeches in front of each other and at home. The remaining children spent one of these sessions listing arguments for and against the topic and in the second, each child adopted a persona for the public meeting. They were to determine their individual position on the topic and prepare one or two questions to ask at question time. On the day of the forum the speakers brought appropriate clothes to school to dress in the role of the character they were playing.

One of the teachers, as master of ceremonies, began by welcoming everyone quite formally and outlining how the program would be conducted (Regulatory). Each speaker had a maximum of three minutes. Following the six individual presentations, members of the audience could ask any relevant questions or express their points of view. Those who spoke from the floor would be required to identify themselves and declare any vested interest they had in the issue (Personal).

Here is the speech prepared by Jessica, who spoke in the role of the Coca-Cola Company representative.

Coca Cole Representative

Hello. I'm a rep from Coca Cola.

Firstly the Company never said that the children had to drink Coca Cola, we only said that the school had to show the symbol around the school. We also wanted to have our name on the camp.

We do have caffeine in our drink but so do lots of other drinks. Caffeine is legal and doesn't have many side effects, unlike other drugs. We are helping poor parents pay for their kids to go to camp. This is a once in a life time offer. Have you ever had coke or coffee before? Have you ever allowed your child to drink coke? Then why are you against our offer? Sure if a drug is legal, that doesn't always mean it is always okay but coke has passed all the tests. We have enough money as it is and if you don't want this offer, it's no loss to us. It's not often that big companies like us, come down to small schools like yours and offer you money. We are doing it out of kindness of our company's heart but we can't just give you the money. There has to be a reason. We are not making you take coke or "the caffeine fix" as you like to call it, we just want our name on the camp or a logo on your school. We wouldn't give primary school children our drink if it wasn't okay.

The school council has the last say in this matter. If they say "No" some children's families may not be able to afford the camp cost and therefore may not be able to go on camp. If they say "Yes" then the children will be able to go on camp and enjoy themselves. The choice is yours.

—JESSICA

The children's speeches presented examples of personal language (introduction and biographical information), divertive language (some children made puns of their names or included some jokes in their presentations), representational language (provided information through their reasoning), toward logical reasoning (recognized causal and dependent relationships and drew conclusions), and imaginative language (envisioned a world without drugs and Coca-Cola).

This forum provides an opportunity for some of the students to make a formal presentation in front of a relatively large audience. They have practice in writing a speech: how to begin by introducing their position; how to present supporting reasons; and how to make a conclusion that packs a punch. All children have further experience of argumentative language, of identifying reasons to support either side of an issue. Many have the opportunity to learn how to ask questions at a public meeting.

All these argumentative language sessions are providing time for the children to process new information they have taken on board, and in so doing make greater sense of it. Importantly, they are becoming competent in the language of argument. Such competence is necessary for those intent on speaking out and addressing social inequalities.

Applying Knowledge: Saying "No" to Drugs

The initial focus of the study was the type of information needed to be able to make informed decisions about drugs. The unit of study then focused on strategies to minimize drug use, such as how to resist peer pressure. Children worked in small groups listing the many different responses they could give if ever pressured into taking drugs or into doing anything against their will.

Situation: Someone Wants You to Take a Drug

"I'll save it for when I'm really feeling bad."

"I've had them before and they upset my stomach."

Say, "Maybe later," and never come back.

Take them off the person, walk away and then throw them in the nearest bin without people seeing you.

Walk away like you didn't hear.

Say "No thanks." Walk away and blend into the crowd.

"No thanks. I've heard they make pizza taste bad and I'm having pizza tonight."

"Have you had some before? Did it have any side effects?"

Situation: Covering Up for Someone

"It's not my problem. Deal with it yourself.'

"No thanks," and walk away.

"I'm sick of getting in trouble."

"I'm busy now. Ask someone else."

Ignore them and walk away.

Change the subject.

"I can't help you. Ask . . ." (another person)

The application of this knowledge is constantly on the agenda in the children's classroom lives. The teachers are alert to situations that happen in the classroom and schoolyard where the children have opportunities to try these strategies. In other words, the application of learning is ongoing.

Evaluating Knowledge: Reflecting on Learning

At the end of the unit , all the children were asked to reflect by writing to the following four prompts (Figure 5–1):

I never knew that . . .

I've changed my mind about . . .

The most important thing I'll remember . . .

I'm still wondering about . . .

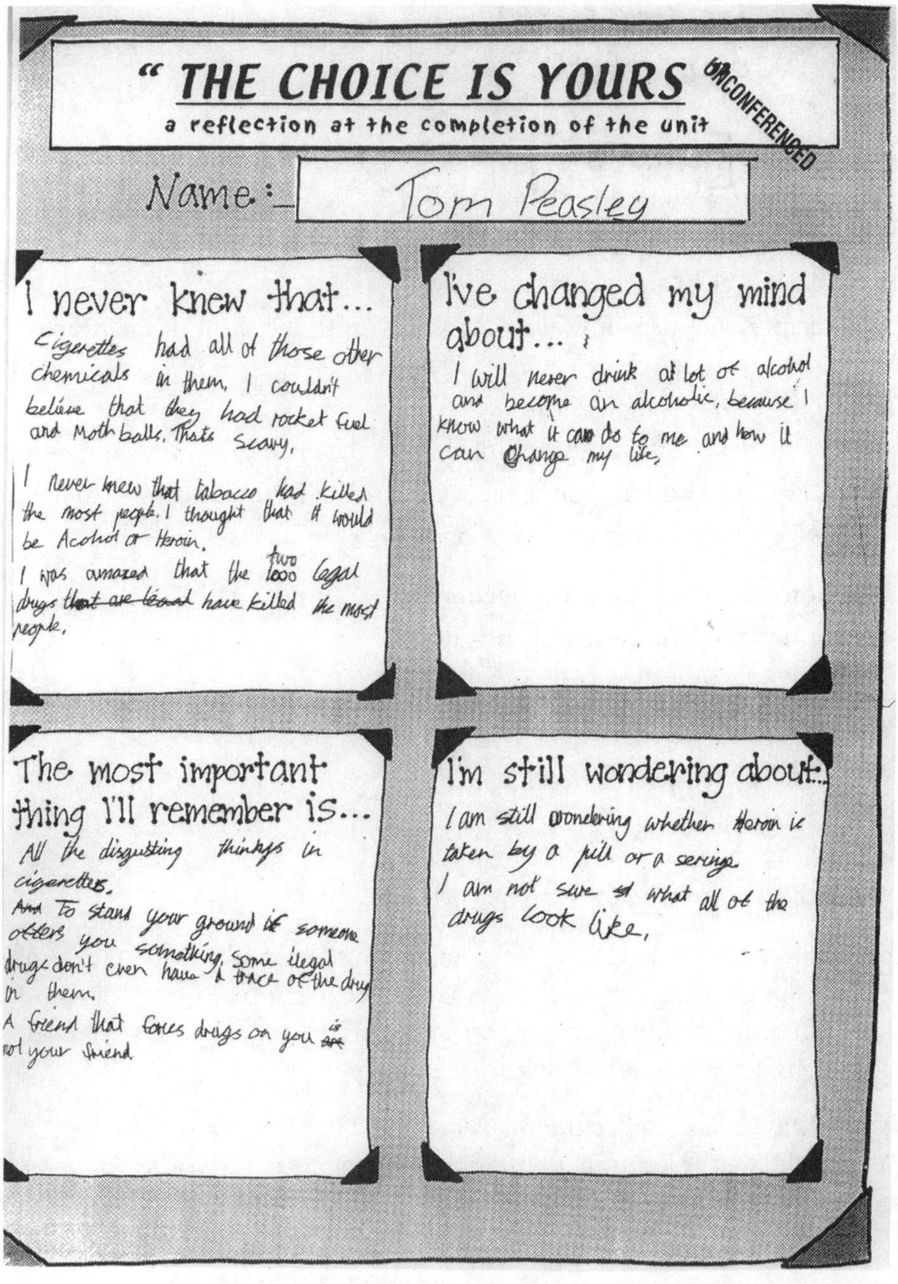

" THE CHOICE IS YOURS

a reflection at the completion of the unit

6thCONFERENCED

Name: __Tom Peasley__

I never knew that...

Cigerettes had all of those other chemicals in them. I couldn't believe that they had rocket fuel and Moth balls. That's scary,

I never knew that tabacco had killed the most people. I thought that it would be Acohol or Heroin.

I was amazed that the two 1000 legal drugs that are leagal have killed the most people.

I've changed my mind about...

I will never drink a lot of alcohol and become an alcoholic, because I know what it can do to me and how it can change my life.

The most important thing I'll remember is...

All the disgusting things in cigerettes.

And to stand your ground if someone offers you something. Some ilegal drugs don't even have a trace of the drug in them.

A friend that forces drugs on you is not your friend

I'm still wondering about...

I am still wondering whether Heroin is taken by a pill or a seringe

I am not sure of what all of the drugs look like.

Figure 5–1   Tom's Reflections at the End of the Unit on Drugs

Through this integrated study, children were busy using language for a wide range of purposes as they learned about drugs. They were improving their listening, speaking, writing, and reading skills as they investigated various elements of the inquiry, and learning more about language itself—to conduct the formal meetings of a forum or to structure a written argument. Language and learning were inextricably intertwined.

Wondering About the World

Bag Lady

She
came toward me
on the footpath
old and grey and stooped.
Her life possessions packed
in two plastic carrying bags.
Though the day was warm
she wore her wardrobe
a winter hat
and long woollen coat
over several layers of clothes.
Bag lady.
What was her past?
What is her future?

—LORRAINE WILSON

If we want to realize our visions of a more just society we need to get tomorrow's citizens thinking now about current social issues and teach them to imagine or pose alternatives. A regular "wondering session" provides an opportunity for children to explore hot issues and to think of other ways of being through writing.

In one such session with a grade 5–6 double unit, I first discussed with the children some of my concerns about the world today: wars, greed, starvation. I went on to say I felt it important for them to think about these issues and to know that the world doesn't have to be as it is. We compiled a list of hot issues that we would take time to write about:

war	pollution	drought	global warming
looting	homelessness	wildlife	bullying
disease	terrorism		

Bullying

A quick show of hands from the children settled bullying as the topic of the first wondering session. With no preliminary discussion, the children settled in to write their individual thoughts on bullying. When finished, they shared and discussed the issues in small groups.

Being bullied is what every little kid at school fears. Even older children are scared of being teased or hurt. When people think about bullies, they think of big mean bossy people. We think that bullying is wrong—and it is. But do people ever think why it happens? Why do bullies push you around and insult you? Maybe it is because they are just mean people, but I also think, that in every situation, there are deeper reasons. Bullies may scare you, but inside they are probably the ones that are scared and afraid. They've probably been excluded from a group or bullied in some form. Perhaps they have problems at home like parents getting divorced or a relative dying.

—LEXIE

Note how Lexie, through writing, hypothesizes about why bullies behave as they do.

I wonder what life would be like without bullying. Big countries wouldn't try to push little countries around and there wouldn't be any war. Every kid would be happy at school and there would be no racism, everyone would be happy. No-one would force anyone to take drugs if they didn't want to and adults couldn't force kids to do their homework or set the table. White people couldn't make black people fell ashamed of the shade of their skin or their culture. No-one would make fun of the way someone looks and no-one would get their feelings hurt. And most important of all no-one would waste their lives being a bully. What a world it would be without bullying.

—LUKE

Luke fantasizes about what the world would be like without bullying.

Tomorrow, another day, another time, another event. Who knows what could happen, maybe bullying might disappear. Maybe racism would stop, or abuse would never be heard of again.

Bullying is everyone's problem, even if you are not the victim. Whoever you are, whatever you do, you can help stop the misery that bullying causes.

Bullying doesn't go anywhere, it doesn't take you away from where you are, it doesn't prove anything. All it causes is someone else's depression.

—PAIGE

Paige tries to find a solution by challenging all of us to help stop bullying.

Homelessness

On another day the wondering topic was homelessness.

Homelessness

I say that the world is quite uneven in that some people have everything and other people have nothing at all, not even a house.

Most of my friends have their own rooms. I'm sure all homeless people want is a real bed, mattress, quilt, pillow and a roof over they're heads.

I wonder how they came to be at that bus-stop? Was it their fault? Did they run away from home? I would hate to wander the streets all day, sleep on the ground all night.

There are so many questions to ask.

—EVELYN

Homelessness

Imagine not having a home to go to at night. Not having a bed to sleep in. Not having a roof over your head. Personally I don't think it's fair. Everyone should have a fair shot at life and not be thrown in the gutter and forgotten about. These people have dreams to. They are the same as you or me. The only difference is *we* have food, *we* have a bed and *we* have opportunities.

Every night we go home, eat our hot meals then curl up in our beds with pillows and blankets.

—ALEX

Homelessness

Homelessness must be impossible to handle. Imagine living with no shelter and no cozy bed to go home to. Many turn to crime to gain a small amount of money to rent a house.

One reason people are homeless is they are unemployed. Homelessness is only going to increase if companies keep cutting jobs at the current rate.

—DAN

The Value of Required Wondering Topics

In all these pieces children use language to represent the world; some use it to challenge the world today and others pose alternate ways of being. Writers incorporate many of Smith's and Tough's language use classifications included in Chapter 4. Through writing the children address the larger world out there. In classroom discussions, children air different points of view, seek solutions, and believe that they can make a difference.

During personal writing time children choose the topics they write about. We find that topics addressed in the required writing strand, such as the wonder topics, can trigger some of the choices made by the children at personal writing time. Following the class exploration of the topic bullying, Sandra chose her personal writing time to start a whole new piece about bullying and wrote extensively on the issue. I include just one small segment of her writing here.

> There is another type of bullying, it is racism. Racism is a type of teasing about the color of your skin. It is so annoying and unthinkable that somebody can brag about your color. It is not your fault what your color is and you were born like that, or were in a different country. I wish that everyone who's a different color to you or you from them, can just not worry and live very peacefully and be smiling all the time.
>
> —SANDRA, GRADE 5–6

Writing Social Narrative

In personal writing time Lexie chose to write about the Stolen Generation. Until the 1960s, the Australian government officials forcibly removed children from their Aboriginal parents, particularly those children with a lighter skin color, and kept them in orphanages. Many never saw their families again. Those children are known now as the "Stolen Generation." The last decade in Australia has seen much publicity of the social dislocation, pain, and suffering caused by this government policy.

In Lexie's classroom the Stolen Generation is another social issue addressed through literature, poems, and class discussions. In writing this fictional piece Lexie is projecting herself into the thoughts of a mother who has lost her child and in so doing, is trying to understand her grief and suffering.

The Stolen Generation.

"NOOOOOOO, GIVE HER BACK! YOU'RE NOT ALLOWED TO TAKE HER AWAY FRROM ME. SHE WANTS TO LIVE HERE WITH ME!"
I scream and scream until my voice is hoarse and my lungs feel like their burning. Then I cry. I cry until there are no more tears left in my body. How dare they take my daughter away from me. How dare they deny me of my own child. Anger swells inside me like hot lave bubbling in my body, filling me with hatred for those horrible heartbreaking White People. I try to release my anger, kicking at the ground and yelling like crazy, but all that resulted in, was me getting a sore foot, and all my family and friends coming to see what the matter was.

"Anna, Anna, what is wrong?"
They speak in our language urgently, glancing from me and to the bush around—looking for my precious daughter.
"They took our little Alice—they stole her." I hear my voice stuttering and waves of new fear wash over me.
"She's gone and I'll never see her again."
Fresh tears spill down my cheeks like miniature rivers.
"Why do the White People do this? Why do they think we're bad parents?" I ask, hoping someone will have a good enough answer.
"Because they're dumb and selfish," replies my best friend Lilly in a hollow voice.
"But don't worry Anna," she adds, trying to sound confident, "We'll see Alice again, somewhere, somehow, someday."
I sniff in response, willing myself to believe her, though I know she doesn't even believe it herself.
Maybe, just maybe I'll see Alice again. And if I do, I will never part with her until I die.

—LEXIE, GRADE 6

Lee Heffernan and Mitzi Lewison (2003) coined the term *social narrative* to describe a genre where students create fictional worlds drawing on shared cultural resources and where they use the writing to both construct and analyze these social worlds. Social narrative is social action. So personal writing, a time when individual children select their own topics and have the opportunity to review and reflect on their own worlds, can be a time when individual children address key social issues through the fictional worlds they create. Like Lexie, children take on some of the world's great injustices in simple narratives.

Integrating Children's Lives into the Classroom

Integrating the learning of language with learning about the world does not mean just integrating studies of class topics. More broadly, it means children using language to learn more about themselves, their families, and their communities. It means integrating their lives into the class program. What children learn about or make sense of in class time comes both from their individual contexts and from shared contexts as a community (see Figure 5–2).

In Chapter 1, I wrote about the need to value children if we are to aim for a more caring, just society. Valuing our students means welcoming them and their lives into our classrooms. It means ensuring that every student in the classroom, not only the brightest, is represented in classroom displays. It means providing class time for them to talk and write about themselves, their interests, their hopes, their worries. When children write

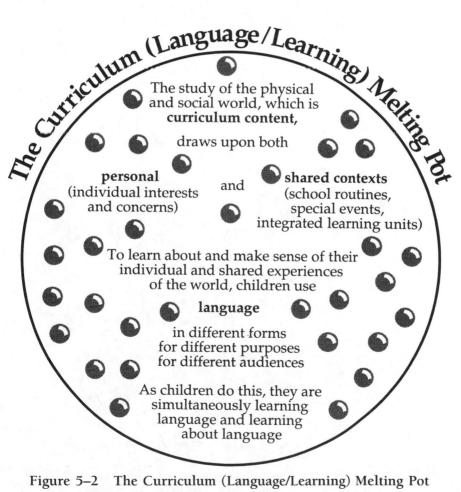

The study of the physical and social world, which is **curriculum content,** draws upon both

personal (individual interests and concerns)   and   **shared contexts** (school routines, special events, integrated learning units)

To learn about and make sense of their individual and shared experiences of the world, children use

language

in different forms for different purposes for different audiences

As children do this, they are simultaneously learning language and learning about language

Figure 5–2   The Curriculum (Language/Learning) Melting Pot
(Wilson et al. 1991, 11)

about personal concerns teachers gain insight into what their needs are and the children gain a greater understanding of issues impacting them by externalizing them. Classroom planning should include regular sessions where children choose the topic and form of what they write and read.

Imogen's family went through traumatic times with the death of a much-loved three-year-old nephew. Imogen chose to write about him in a personal writing session (see Figure 5–3). Imogen's sensitive, caring teacher has made a note of extra information learned from Imogen while conferencing her piece.

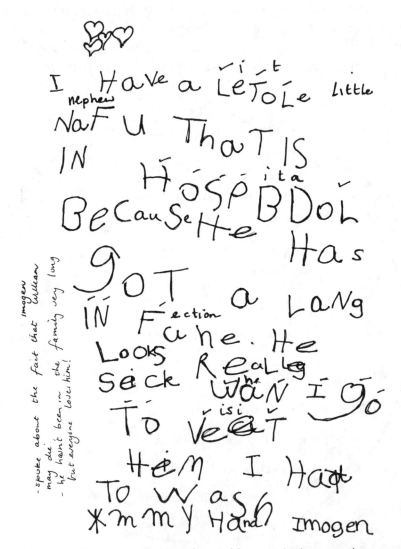

I have a little nephew that is in hospital because he has got a lung infection. He looks really sick. When I go to visit him I had to wash my hands.

Figure 5–3

Classroom Practice

Tapping Children's Existing Knowledge

Children Ask Questions   If learning is to start with the children and their existing knowledge, many of the questions they investigate should be their own. Jenny Hodges asked her K–2 children at the start of a study of dinosaurs what they wanted to find out. Look at first-grader Jacinta's questions (Figure 5–4). She even wants to know what dinosaurs look like inside their bodies.

Children Sketch Life Cycles or Processes   When investigating some living thing from the plant or animal world children can tap their existing knowledge by drawing a life cycle.

In Figure 5–5, note Freya's understanding of the life cycle of a tree. In the same classroom a younger child began his life cycle with a tree stump. For him at that time, the life of a tree began with a tree stump. It is important for the class teacher to be alert to different children's understandings of the same issue.

A similar useful activity is to have children trace the process involved in the making of something being studied; for example, jeans, or milk. Note also Claire's explanation of the workings of a hair dryer in Figure 5–6.

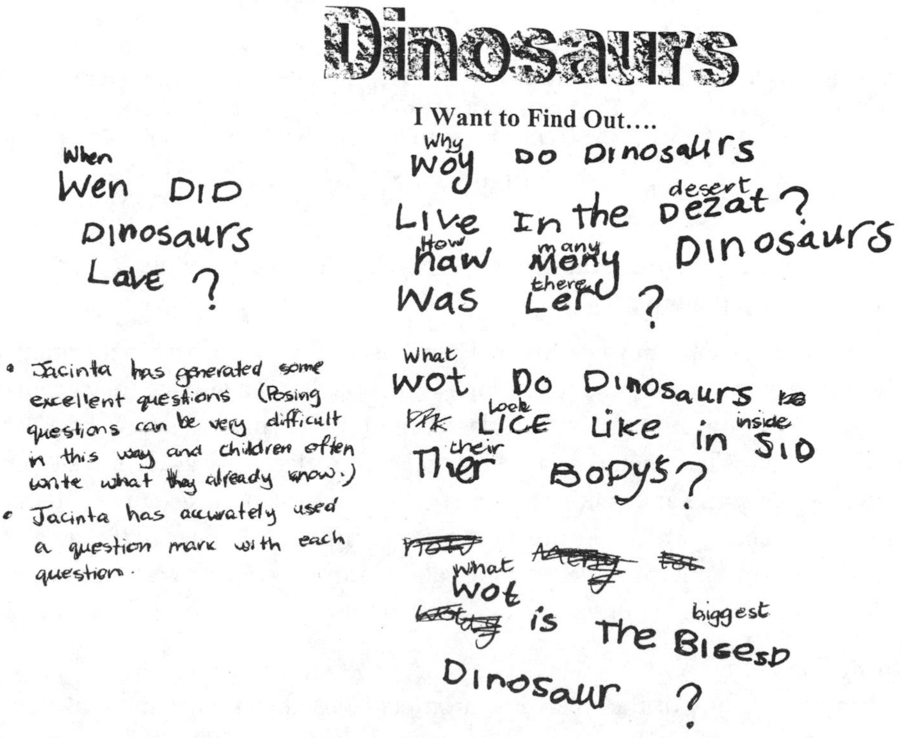

Dinosaurs

I Want to Find Out....

When
Wen DID
Dinosaurs
Lave ?

Why
Woy Do Dinosaurs
Live In the Dezat (desert) ?
How many there
haw mony Dinosaurs
Was Left ?

What
Wot Do Dinosaurs
look inside
PPk LICE Like in Sid
their
Ther Bodys?

what
Wot biggest
is The Bisesp
Dinosaur ?

• Jacinta has generated some excellent questions (Posing questions can be very difficult in this way and children often write what they already know.)

• Jacinta has accurately used a question mark with each question.

Figure 5–4

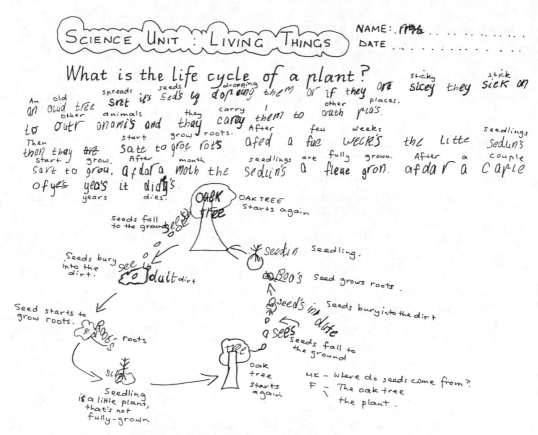

An old tree spreads its seeds dropping them or if they are sticky they stick on to other animals and they carry them to other places. Then they start to grow roots. After a few weeks the little seedlings start to grow. After a month the seedlings are fully grown. After a couple of years it dies.

Figure 5–5

Write Statements of Existing Knowledge Individually children write sentences about what they know on the topic.

Brainstorm and Group Words In small groups, children cooperatively brainstorm all the words they can think of about a topic. When the list is complete they group their words and label them. In a grade 4–5 class beginning an investigation about energy, almost all the groups had many, many words related to electricity as a source of energy. But knowledge of renewable sources of energy was almost nonexistent, evidenced by the absence of related words on their brainstorming lists. The teachers, as a result, planned to develop understanding of renewable and nonrenewable sources of energy and, specifically, knowledge of wind and solar power.

Evaluating Learning

Teachers might use any of the following prompts to establish what the children have learned.

Clare

Write/ draw/label all the stages involved for a particular appliance to operate

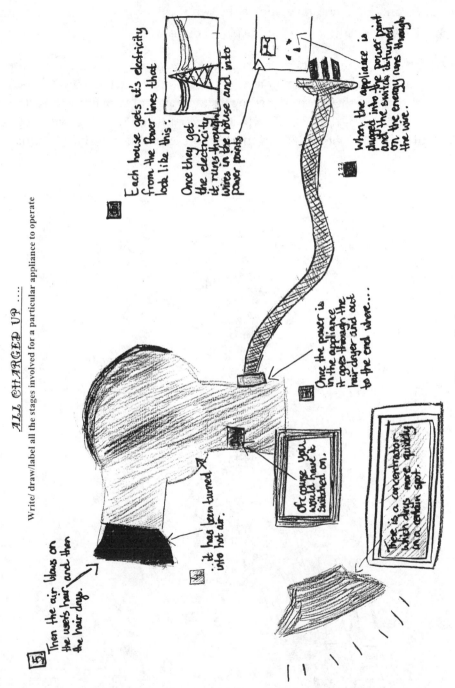

5. Then the air blows on the users hair and then the hair drys.

..it has been turned into hot air.

Of course you would have it switched on.

Here is a concentrator which drys more quickly in a certain spot.

Once the power is in the appliance it goes through the hair dryer and out to the end where....

Each house gets it's electricity from the Power lines that look like this :

Once they get the electricity it runs through wires in the house and into power points

When the appliance is plugged into the power point and the switch is turned on the energy runs through the wire.

Figure 5–6

1. Children write, "What I have learned?"
2. Children draw a life cycle of a butterfly, for example, and later draw a second life cycle and compare the two.
3. Draw and label a system to explain how it works.

Di Woodburn and Mandy Jones team teach a K–2 group of children. At the conclusion of an integrated investigation of the body, they asked each of the students to draw the inside of their body, labelling each organ and explaining how the body worked (see Figures 5–7, 5–8). The children's completed drawings were placed in their cumulative assessment files together with the necessary contextual data (see Figure 5–9).

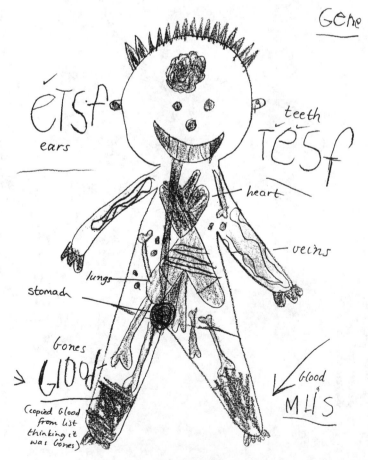

Figure 5–7

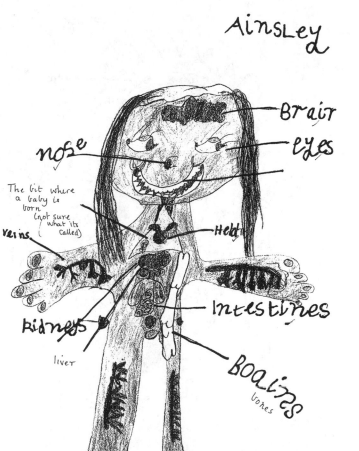

Ainsley

Brain
eyes
nose
The bit where
a baby is
born
(not sure
what its
called)
veins
Held
Intestines
kidneys
liver
BOALing
bones

Figure 5–8

Diaries

Diaries, used in many K–2 rooms to record personal thoughts, feelings, and activities, are a vehicle for children to bring their lives into the classroom. I'm inclined to think a weekly entry is sufficient. I have seen the daily entry become tedious and heard some children complaining, "We don't know what to write."

Of course, it helps if the teacher also keeps a diary. Very large, blank-page books are good for use as the teacher's diary because the writing can be large enough for all children to read. The teacher demonstrates the type of entries that are made in diaries, and shows that diary writing is one-draft writing. Children should be free to take entries from their diaries and develop these further at personal writing time.

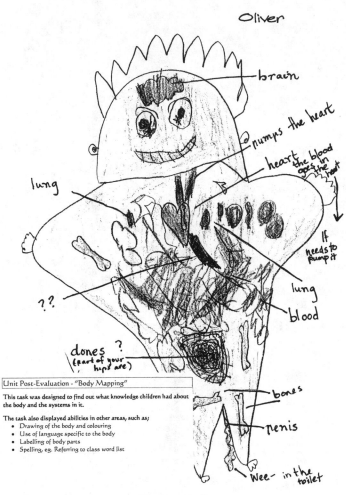

Oliver

brain

pumps the heart

heart
the blood
goes in
the heart

lung

If
needs to
pump it

lung

blood

?.?.

bones ?
(part of your
hips are)

Unit Post-Evaluation - "Body Mapping"

This task was designed to find out what knowledge children had about
the body and the systems in it.

The task also displayed abilities in other areas, such as;
- Drawing of the body and colouring
- Use of language specific to the body
- Labelling of body parts
- Spelling, eg. Referring to class word list

bones

penis

Wee- in the
toilet

Figure 5–9

Class Diary

This is not a personal diary but a diary of the activities of the class and as such helps
build classroom community. It is a joint construction, scribed by the teacher with all
students contributing. Weekly entries work well for this, too, with Friday being a good
day to make entries. Much fun can be had in writing up class happenings. At the end
of each term the diary can be typed and a copy given to each child to keep. A published copy, with artwork by the students, is kept in the classroom.

Letter Diaries

Letter diaries are kept in exercise books. One exercise book is the joint property of both
one child and the teacher. The teacher writes a letter to each child, perhaps once a week
or, if time is an issue, once every two weeks. The child writes back. This is an excellent
way to develop trusting relationships between teachers and students. The teachers write
of their lives and families and so do the children. When trust is established students

use the letter diaries to raise issues of concern to them, sometimes school related and sometimes related to out-of-school matters. Initially, some students may write very little, particularly if teachers write lots of questions to be answered. When students understand that this is a vehicle for genuine two-way communication, they begin to write more (Figures 5–10 and 5–11).

Letters

A school postal system can prompt children to write to one another and to teachers. All that is needed is a school post box and volunteers to empty the box and sort and deliver the letters once a day. Teachers can use the school postal system to write letters to some children who need a little bit of encouragement.

Yearbooks

Yearbooks have been part of the program at Moonee Ponds West Primary School for several decades. They are introduced in grade 5–6 and are a record of major class and local events during that year. Each month the teachers design a Month Page (e.g., August Page) and all children are required to make choices from that page and complete a double-page entry in their yearbooks. The entries combine art and writing. The yearbooks become a record of the children's last two years at primary school as well as an avenue for trying out different presentation and art techniques, which may later be used in larger publishing ventures. The children become very attached to their yearbooks.

Some time is allowed in class for completion of each month's entry but work is also sometimes done at home to meet the deadline for having the entry completed. Occasionally there is an invitation for parents to join in an activity—as happened on the August Page during the drug unit of investigation (See Figure 5–12 on page 100). Note on the August Page that the teachers have included two school issues; the introduction of Book Club and safety on the school playground. This is one way children can be involved in the decision making of issues that affect them. This is democracy in action in classrooms.

Literature Sets

Children worry about issues such as war and homelessness. Even though they may have no direct experience of such issues, they hear daily references to them on the radio and television. At this current time war takes up much air time and fourth-, fifth-, and sixth-grade teachers have noticed more children are choosing to write about war.

The War We Couldn't Win

Gunshots ripped through the night sky like a hot knife through butter. Curses and screams of agony could be heard from afar. Dirt clods flew as missiles thudded into the earth. An assortment of weapons lay on the ground, left there by people fleeing the Machines, who knew no fear. Bullets sank into the soft metal of the machines hardly even making them falter.

Engines screamed overhead raining death from above. We were losing the war and we knew it!

—PATRICK

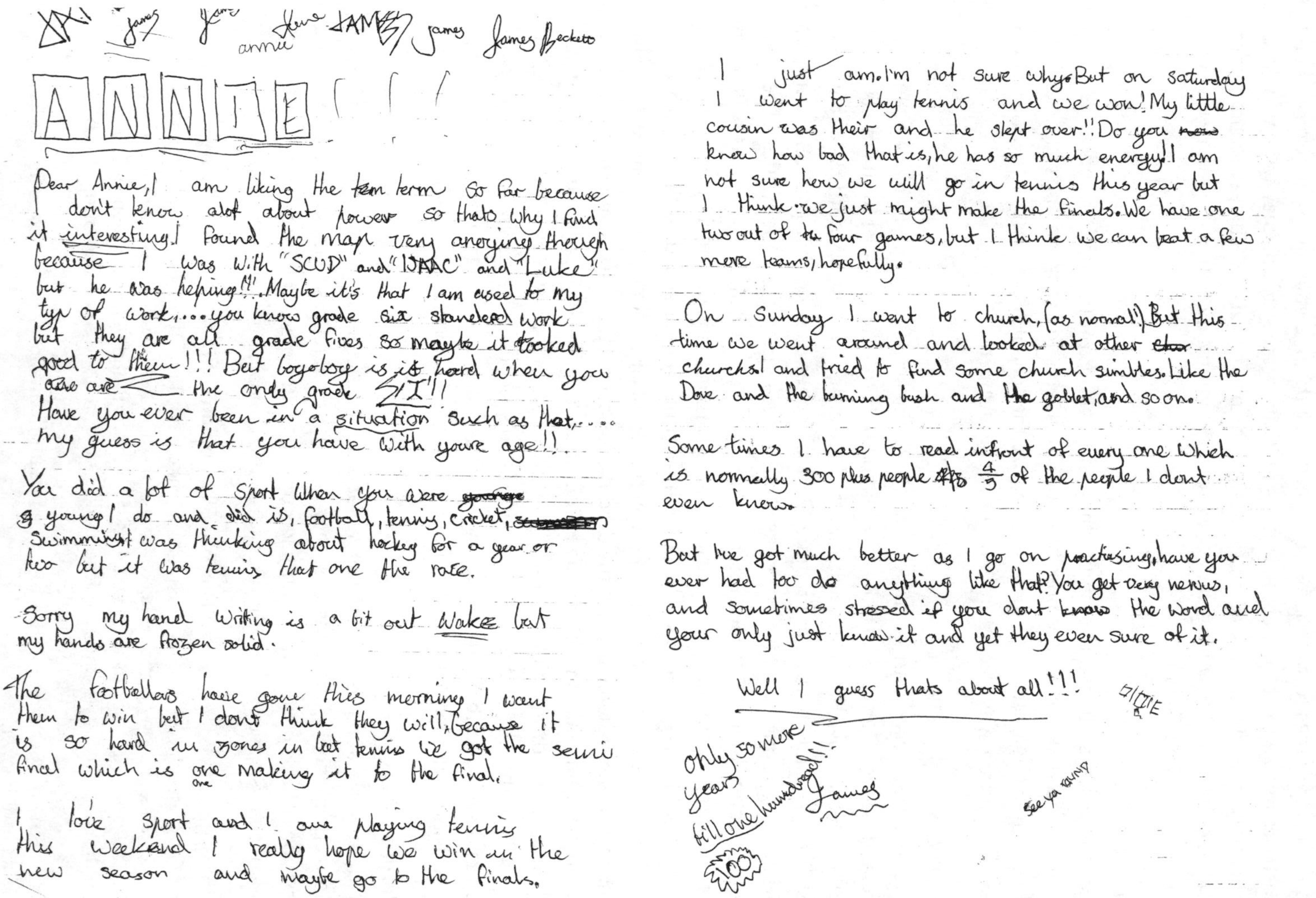

Dear Annie, I am liking the term so far because I don't know a lot about tennis so that's why I find it interesting! Found the map very annoying through because I was with "SCUD" and "DAAC" and Luke but he was helping. Maybe it's that I am excel to my try of work... you know grade six standard work but they are all grade fives so maybe it looked good to them!!! But biology is it hard when you are the only grade 7?!!! Have you ever been in a situation such as that.... my guess is that you have with your age!!

You did a lot of sport when you were young! I do and did is football, tennis, cricket, swimming! was thinking about hockey for a year or two but it was tennis that one the race.

Sorry my hand writing is a bit out. Wakee left my hands are frozen solid.

The footballers have gone this morning I want them to win but I don't think they will, because it is so hard in zones in last tennis we got the semi final which is are making it to the final.

I love sport and I am playing tennis this weekend. I really hope we win on the new season and maybe go to the finals.

I just am. I'm not sure why. But on saturday went to play tennis and we won. My little cousin was their and he slept over. Do you know how bad that is, he has so much energy. I am not sure how we will go in tennis this year but I think we just might make the finals. We have one two out of the four games, but I think we can beat a few more teams, hopefully.

On Sunday I went to church (as normal). But this time we went around and looked at other churches and tried to find some church similar. Like the Dove and the burning bush and the goblet and so on.

Sometimes I have to read in front of every one which is normally 300 plus people $\frac{4}{5}$ of the people I don't even knows.

But I've got much better as I go on practising. Have you ever had to do anything like that? You got any news, sometimes stressed if you don't know the word and your only just knows it and yet they even sure of it.

Well I guess that's about all!!!!

only so more year!!!

James

Figure 5–10 James' Letter to Annie, His Teacher

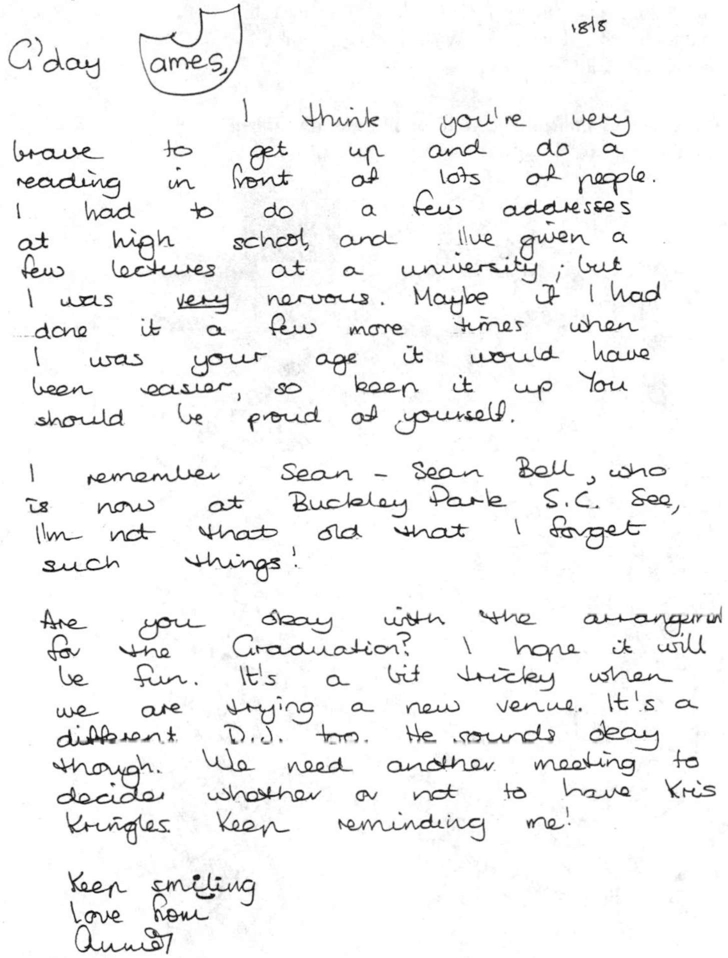

G'day James,

1818

I think you're very brave to get up and do a reading in front of lots of people. I had to do a few addresses at high school, and I've given a few lectures at a university; but I was very nervous. Maybe if I had done it a few more times when I was your age it would have been easier, so keep it up You should be proud of yourself.

I remember Sean – Sean Bell, who is now at Buckley Park S.C. See, I'm not that old what I forget such things!

Are you okay with the arrangements for the Graduation? I hope it will be fun. It's a bit tricky when we are trying a new venue. It's a different D.J. too. He sounds okay though. We need another meeting to decide whether or not to have Kris Kringles Keep reminding me!

Keep smiling
Love from
Annie

Figure 5–11   Annie's Reply

Such issues can and need to be discussed in classrooms. Today there are excellent novels written for eleven- and twelve-year-old students on the topic of war. Class sets (six to eight copies) can be purchased so that it is possible for everyone in a class to be reading a variety of novels on one topic. Later, everyone can discuss in small groups and share what they have learned and what they are left wondering about. Some suggested books are included in the reference section below.

Summary: Learning Language as We Learn the World

In any one language event children can be learning to use language, learning by using language, and learning about language. Shared classroom investigations include hot issues of the day such as drugs, bullying, and homelessness. If in our classrooms we

At the moment we are trying to decide whether Bookclub
should be offered at M.P.W. What is your opinion? Give
detailed reasons!

Or

Lots of time has been devoted to making our playground safer and more
enjoyable for all. What do you think is the biggest problem and how can we
rectify it?

Figure 5–12   August Page from the Year Book

are working for a fairer world, issues relating to social justice must be addressed. Classroom planning includes time where children are encouraged to investigate personal
interests and concerns.

References

Drug Education K–12 Project, Teacher Support Package Phase 1. 1999. Victoria, Australia: School
    Drug Education Project.

Emmitt, M., J. Pollock, and L. Komesaroff. 2003. *Language and Learning: An Introduction for Teach-
    ing.* 3d ed., New York: Oxford University Press.

Golub, J. N. 2003. "Learn About 'Writing As a Tool for Thinking and Learning.'" *The Council
    Chronicle,* 13 (2): 1, 7.

Heffernan, L., and M. Lewison. 2003. "Social Narrative Writing: (Re)Constructing Kid Culture in the Writer's Workshop." *Language Arts*, 80 (6): 435–43.

Krashen, S. D. 2003. *Explorations in Language Acquisition and Use*. Portsmouth, NH: Heinemann.

Smith, F. 1982. *Writing and the Writer*. London: Heinemann Educational Books.

Tough, J. 1977. *Talking and Learning*. London: Ward Lock Educational.

Wilson, L., D. Malmgren, S. Ramage, and L. Schulz. 1991. *An Integrated Approach to Learning*, South Melbourne: Thomas Nelson Australia.

Children's Novels About War

Ellis, D. 2002a. *Parvana*. Melbourne, Australia: Allen & Unwin.

———. 2002b. *Parvana's Journey*. Melbourne, Australia: Allen & Unwin.

Filipovic, Z. 1994. *Zlata's Diary*. London: Viking.

Frank, A. 1993. *Anne Frank: The Diary of a Young Girl*. New York: Bantam.

French, J. 2003. *Hitler's Daughter*. Pymble: HarperCollins.

Lowry, L. 1989. *Number the Stars*. New York: A Yearling Book.

Mattingley, C. 1993. *No Gun for Asmir*. Melbourne, Australia: Puffin Books.

Warren A. 2001. *Surviving Hitler: A Boy in the Nazi Death Camps*. New York: HarperCollins.

Yolen, J. 1988. *The Devil's Arithmetic*. New York: Puffin Books.

DEVELOPING WRITERS TO WRITE (RIGHT) THE WORLD

I write the world.

I write about
me
my freckles
Dad's bad back.
I write about
Grandma dying.

I write to find out
what makes freckles
where the sun goes at night
how birds fly without falling.
I write to find out
where Grandma is now.

I write to make change
to stop bullying
to keep cats inside
to clean up the rivers
to ask why—
there was no hospital bed for grandma.

I right the world

—LORRAINE WILSON

For children to develop as writers who believe they can write (right) the world, certain classroom conditions apply. These conditions relate to how the child perceives himself in general and how he perceives himself as a learner—both inextricably linked to the nature of the class learning program. Learning programs that ignore individual needs will not develop confident writers. Empowering programs are those that focus on individual student strengths and needs. Empowering programs start where the learners are.

Each Learner Must Believe in Himself and in His Potential to Learn

The teaching learning program begins with each individual learner. Children entering the same classroom are not the same. While there are similarities, children differ—cognitively, emotionally, physically, and culturally.

Class learning programs that build confident learners are accepting of difference and plan for the ongoing learning of each child. The programs begin with each child's existing knowledge and understandings. They set goals appropriate to each child's level of understanding so that success in achievement is possible for each learner. They value and celebrate all children's achievements.

Only by accepting a child and his language will the child have the confidence necessary to take those risks that are so much a part of the language learning process, and specifically of learning to write. Linda Christenson writes,

> When I was in ninth grade Mrs Delaney, my English teacher wanted to demonstrate the correct and incorrect ways to pronounce the English language. She asked Helen Draper, whose father owned several clothing stores in town, to stand and say "lawyer". Then she asked me, whose father owned a bar, to stand and say "lawyer". Everyone burst into laughter at my pronunciation.
>
> What did Mrs Delaney accomplish? Did she make me pronounce "lawyer" correctly? No. I say attorney. I never say lawyer. In fact I've found substitutes for every word my tongue can't get around and for all the rules I can't remember. (2000, 100)

Learning to Listen, Speak, Read, and Write Is an Interactive Process

The four language modes of listening, speaking, reading, and writing are interrelated and interactive in their development, not isolated, separate domains. Carolyn Burke's concept of the linguistic data pool is most useful in coming to understand the nature of this relationship (Harste, Woodward, and Burke 1984). Burke argued that each language user has a linguistic data pool into which all linguistic encounters feed; that is, language used when speaking, listening, reading, and writing is stored together, and it is from this one store we draw when we engage in further listening, speaking, reading, and writing encounters.

Reading and writing, which have to do with written language, are particularly closely interrelated. Each time we read, we learn something about how written language works. Each time we write we draw on knowledge about written texts, learned by reading. Because of this interrelationship between reading and writing, we take care in the selection of class texts. Every book, poster, or magazine found in a classroom is a demonstration of writing. Everything children read informs them about written texts. Therefore, only authentic texts should find their way into classrooms. Controlled vocabulary readers or phonics readers give children an invalid message about the language of real-world books. When asked to write they have every reason to write in the same inauthentic ways.

Here are some texts that may have an authentic purpose for your classroom.

Everyday Classroom Community Texts

Class timetable

Class routines

List of class members

Computer waiting list

Excursion notes

Birthday cards

Graphs of birthdays, hair color, etc.

Recipes

Class rights, responsibilities, and consequences

Rogues' gallery: photos of children with speech balloons

Songs

Popular rhymes, poems

Letters to classmates

Morning news bulletin

Lists of children's questions

Brainstorming charts

Cafeteria lunch menu and prices

Class Published Texts

Class diary

Class photo album—with captions

Class recounts of excursions, daily events

Narrative joint construction

Science experiments

Innovations on rhymes/stories

Favorite poems

Anthology of poems written by children

Popular jokes

Published Texts

Big books of different text types

Poetry anthologies

Fiction of all types including picture storybooks

Factual books

Biographies and autobiographies

Joke books

Newspapers

Dictionaries

Computer texts

Short story collections

Recipe books

Posters, charts

Magazines

Calligraphy books

Reading quality literature to children enriches their ways of using language and introduces new vocabulary, new phrases, and new metaphors for life. Reading literature teaches about writing.

As in Aris' case below, reading can inform character development when writing fiction. By reading fiction we learn about the structure of fiction—ways of beginning; ways of using dialogue; ways of developing suspense. By reading fiction, we learn about the nature of fiction.

QUESTION: Are there particular authors who have influenced the way you write?

LEXIE (AGE ELEVEN): My fiction writing is influenced by Jacqueline Wilson who writes about girls in orphanages, girls with divorced parents and foster Mums.

QUESTION: Are there particular authors who have influenced the way you write?

ARIS (AGE TEN): Tolkien. I really like writing adventure stories. The Fellowship of the Ring and The Two Stories influenced my characters in "The Dark."

Reading literature aloud to students is teaching them about language, about literacy, and about life. Even in the most difficult classrooms children listen quietly when literature is read aloud. If they were not engaged, if they were not being reached in some way, they would not be listening. As teachers we must seize upon children's passion for particular literary texts to teach them about writing. When they are moved by a text or ask for the same story again and again, we can ask them to try and identify what is it about the text that attracts them. Perhaps we start a large classroom chart, "Why These Are Great Books," on which the title of a text is written along with the reasons children give for wanting to hear these same books again and again. I suggest this idea cautiously, for I would not want love of listening to literature to be dampened by children knowing they might have to write afterward. But a class list of why certain texts appeal may provide links for children to consider in framing their own texts.

Language Learning Involves Immersions and Demonstrations

Immersions

Brian Cambourne (1988), in formulating his conditions for learning, studied what it was that makes it possible for young children to commence school competent in oral language. What happens in the preschool years that enables young children to master such a highly complex cognitive activity? Cambourne identified eight conditions present in preschool environments that together facilitate the development of spoken language. One of these is immersion. From birth, infants are surrounded by spoken language. In the labor room and later in the hospital ward, doctors and nurses speak to the parents and to each other. Visitors come and speak to the mother and directly to the newborn infant. When the infant is taken home spoken language continues to surround him. Parents, siblings, and then friends all converse. People on radio and televisions are heard speaking. The child learns that these preschool immersions of spoken language are simultaneously demonstrations of why people speak: the talk is always for a purpose. Babies practice the pitch and rhythmic patterns they hear. In applying Cambourne's model of learning to the acquisition of written language, it follows that children are similarly immersed in all sorts of written language, commencing in the preschool years. The print in which preschool children are immersed relates to the family life practices. Some young children are immersed in the print of religious texts, observing holy books being read by older family members. Most young children today see environmental print of road signs and of advertizing billboards in their local communities. Some preschool children are immersed in texts of sport, both oral and written. They hear the football broadcasts as their parents listen each weekend. They might see the baseball or football stats their dads study after returning from a big game, or watch both parents poring over the sports pages of their local newspaper. Other children are immersed in picture storybook texts and, through these immersions, come to know that storybooks have pictures and print; that the story starts at the front of the book, that the book has a right and a wrong way to be held when being read.

Not one of us can write a particular text without first having experienced it. Classrooms must plan for immersions in the text types we hope to have children write. Whether a child writes a particular text at school has more to do with his prior experiences than with his intelligence. Early literacy programs favor children who come from homes where they have been read to prior to school entry. This is because the texts in which the preschool child has been immersed match those texts expected to be read at school. This would not be of great concern if all children were granted time for immersions in and demonstrations of school-required texts before being expected to read and write them. But the popularity of the standardization movement, where all children of the same age are measured for competency at the same time in the same school literacies, favors certain students while others fail. If the tests included text types favored by alternate community groups, such as hymns or comics, sports records or fast-food menus, different groups of children would experience success.

Demonstrations

> A demonstration is an example of something being done, and how and why it is being done. Most formal school or school like instruction does not consist of meaningful, powerful demonstrations (except in terms of the instructor's own intentions). However, an adult observing a traffic sign, drawing attention to a brand name on a package, or reading a book aloud, is demonstrating the uses of traffic signs, package labelling or books. Each demonstration shows an aspect of the power of written language. (Smith 1984, 149)

We learn to write by reading and by watching others write. In classrooms there is generally one experienced writer for that one group of children: the teacher. It is important, then, that the teacher write in front of the children. While it is essential that student writers be immersed in all sorts of writing by experienced and professional writers, a big responsibility for being a writer/demonstrator rests on the shoulders of the class teacher.

In recent years it has become fashionable to start writing sessions with the teacher modelling. All too often, unfortunately, this modelled writing is inauthentic. It lacks real purpose. I enter classrooms and see the teacher's modelled writing lying crumpled on the classroom floor. Several days later the same modelled writing rests in the same place on the floor, in more crumpled condition. Real writers value the writing they do. If teacher demonstrations are to have a positive impact on student writers' writing, then teachers must value their own writing. Part of valuing writing is putting it to some authentic use. Teachers can demonstrate writing any text type or genre as their students observe; they can write excursion notes, diary reflections, letters to children who are ill, letters to newspapers, signs for the classroom, funny rhymes for the class next door, shopping lists, personal anecdotes, poems, procedures, reminders of things to do, fictional stories, questions about uncertainties—the list is endless. Demonstrations are necessary to inform developing writers about all aspects of the process of composing written texts.

Learning Involves Experimentation and Approximation

Language learning is a developmental process that takes place over time. It involves much experimentation on the part of the learner.

QUESTION: What do you remember about learning to write in your first years at school?
JACQUI (AGE FOURTEEN): I used to really enjoy that 'cos I loved writing stories. So while I was pulling a letter from the alphabet I was thinking of a story. I don't think I knew words had to have certain letters, just any letters. I also remember the first time we wrote I remembered one or two words like "Bob." Kerrie [the teacher] said it

was right. Then "Bob" was a character that featured in a lot of my stories 'cos I knew it was right.

What a child writes and calls "writing" upon entering school will relate directly to his preschool experiences of writing. I recall a five-year-old in his first weeks at school, scribbling not only all over the piece of paper but all over the table as well. Was he being naughty? No. Careful inquiries to his grandmother revealed that this child had never had access to paper or pencils in his preschool years. He had not been to kindergarten. He did not know that he was supposed to confine his drawing to the paper. Children in the first week of school will write in quite different ways. I list some of them here.

- Large circular scribble without left-to-right directionality. The child knows people put marks on paper to send messages or make meaning of some sort.
- Continuous scribble across the page from right to left or from left to right. The child now knows there are certain directional features observed when writing. Ryan used such scribble in writing to tell about a heartfelt family event (Figure 6–1).
- Use of separate invented symbols. In a classroom environment of print script, where letters in words do not touch, the children who have written in continuous scribble start separating the scribble into separate bits. Initially this might be exactly the same loop of scribble repeated right across the page. When the child realizes that writing does not consist of the same symbol again and again, the symbol used will be varied. Nicholas, in his second week at school, has used drawing, pieces of scribble, some separate personal symbols, and some letterlike symbols—all as writing (See Figure 6–2 on page 110). Note too Jessica's writing (See Figure 6–3 on page 111). This is a letter with love kisses to me, her great-aunt.
- Use of letterlike symbols. The more a child is immersed in print and the more opportunity she has to write, the more the symbols she uses will resemble the letters of the alphabet that she sees in the print around her. In Figure 6–4, Jessica has written the alphabet. Note how the symbols are starting to resemble letters and note, too, how the letter *c* is very evident. The letters young children are most familiar with are those in their names.
- Strings of letters. Children who write in strings of letters understand that when people write they do not make up the marks but, rather, draw from a common bank of symbols, namely, the letters of the alphabet. Jim, in his first week at school, is using the letters of the alphabet to write. Note how the letters of his name, *M, I,* and *J,* feature in his writing (See Figure 6–5 on page 112).
- Groups of letters. When a child understands that in writing words do not touch, or that there are intermittent spaces throughout the writing, he will start separating the symbols or letters he is using into small groups so the writing appears to be set out in words. Sometimes this happens before the child makes any

I love my Grandma so much and their dog died and I loved them
so much and my Mum and Dad and whole family were sad. Ryan

Figure 6–1

sound/letter connections; sometimes this comes after the child has started using letters to represent certain sounds. Some children put dots or lines, rather
than spaces, between their words to indicate their awareness that in writing,
words do not touch. Jarrod's piece in Figure 6–6 on page 113 has the concept
of a word very well established.

• Strings of letters with some sound/letter relationships. This is a significant development. The extra knowledge displayed by the child here is that writers do not use
just any randomly chosen letters in spelling a word, but that the letters used sometimes relate to the sounds heard. Initially the child will represent only the first
consonantal sound heard, in just some of the words.

me   and   my   dad   are   going   shopp
                                          -ing.
Mummy   and   Joshua   are   staying   home-

Figure 6–2

In Figure 6–7 on page 114, Natasha is making many sound/letter connections. The first two lines read: "Mini beasts are important to me/Grasshoppers can only jump with the back legs." Note at the end of Line 2, she has used "B" and "L" for "back" and "legs." Children writing like this will generally represent more letter/sounds early in the piece of writing rather than further on, when they are tiring. Note in this example that Natasha ran out of space when she reached the bottom of the page so she continued down the extreme left-hand side of the page. This also illustrates how children in the early stages of writing are not fully cognizant of spatial issues: where does the writing go when a page is full?

If the teacher wishes to see how much phonic understanding a writer has, it is necessary to have the child read his writing before he forgets what he has written. The

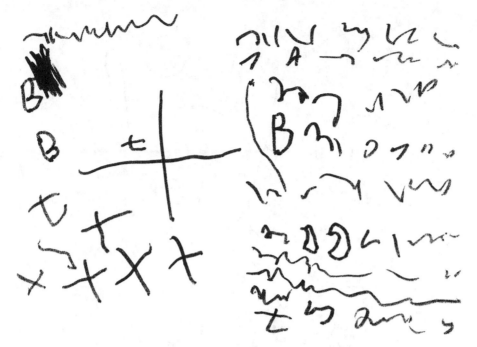

Figure 6–3 Jessica's Letter (four-and-a-half years old)

Figure 6–4 Jessica's Alphabet

— I   miss   mum   when

I'm   at   school.

Figure 6–5

teacher might ask the child to read back at the completion of each sentence, or each line of writing. Doing this, the teacher is often pleasantly surprised at how many letter/ sound associations the child is making. If a child has written a long piece and comes to read it to the teacher, and if she has made only some sound/letter associations (that is, the writing is not yet readable), her oral rendition may well vary from the written version. She has forgotten exactly what she has written, so those sound/letter discoveries are lost.

Teachers need to be alert to some of the common experiments young writers make when cracking the sound/symbol relationships of the English language. Sometimes their writing will reflect their speech: a "d" or "th," as in "den" for "then." Sometimes they use a letter name for a letter sound: "mi" for "my"; "kam" for "came." Sometimes the

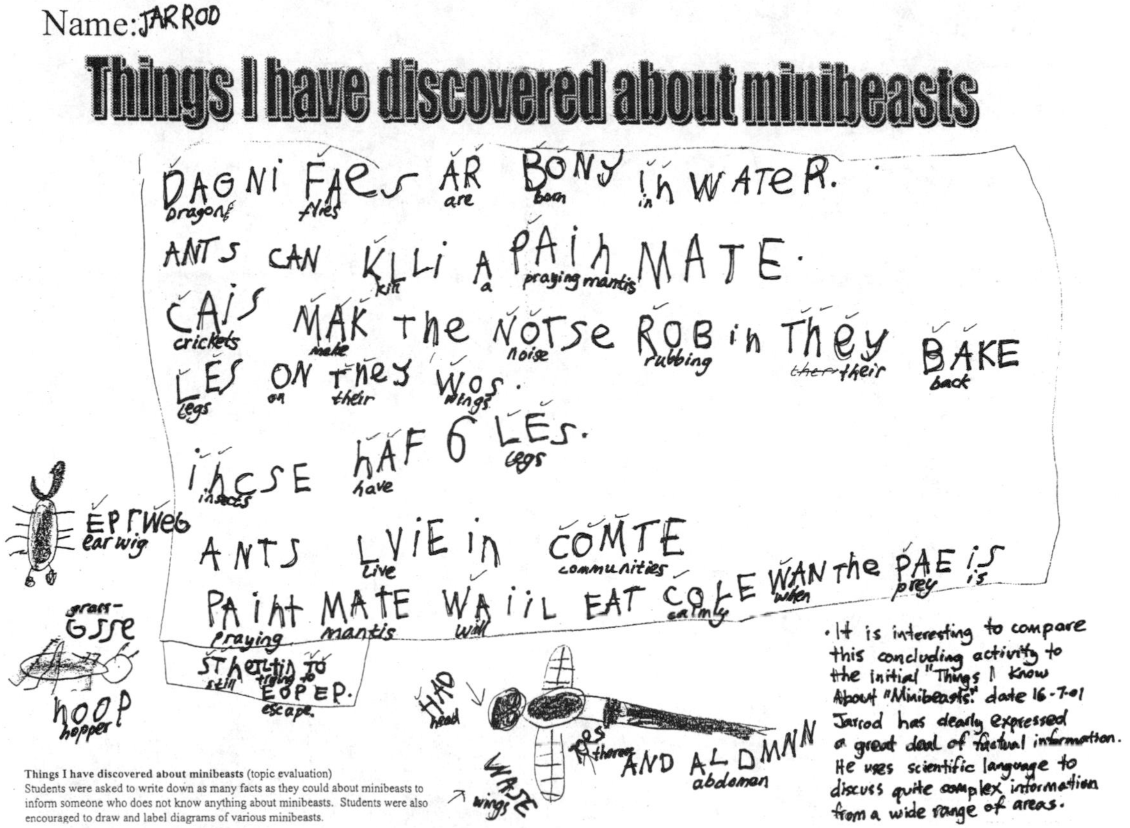

Name: JARROD

Things I have discovered about minibeasts

DAGNI FAEs AR BONY in WATER.
Dragon *flies* *are* *born*

ANTS CAN KLLi A PAiЛ MATE.
kill *a* *praying mantis*

CAiS MAK The NOTSe ROB in THEy BAKE
crickets *make* *noise* *rubbing* *their/their* *back*

LÉS ON THEy Wos.
legs *on* *their* *wings*

iЛCSE hAF 6 LÉS.
insects *have* *legs*

EPrweb
ear wig

ANTS LViE in COMTE
live *communities*

GSSE
grass-hopper

PAiЛt MATE WAiiL EAT COLE WAN the PAE iS
praying mantis *will* *eatmly/calmly* *when* *prey* *is*

hooP
hopper

STЛ outing to
EOP EP.
still *trying to* *escape.*

HAD
head

AND AL DMЛN
abdomen

WЛTE
wings

Things I have discovered about minibeasts (topic evaluation)
Students were asked to write down as many facts as they could about minibeasts to
inform someone who does not know anything about minibeasts. Students were also
encouraged to draw and label diagrams of various minibeasts.

• It is interesting to compare
this concluding activity to
the initial "Things I know
About Minibeasts" date 16-7-01
Jarrod has clearly expressed
a great deal of factual information.
He uses scientific language to
discuss quite complex information
from a wide range of areas.

Things I have Discovered About Mini Beasts
Dragon flies are born in water.
Ants can kill a praying mantis.
Crickets make the noise rubbing their back legs on their wings.
Ants live in communities.
Praying mantis will eat calmly when the prey is still trying to escape.
Jarrod

Figure 6–6

letter name used is an approximation to the sound heard: the letter name "e" for the first sound of "it." The child writes "et" for "it" and "pen" for "pin." The child is hearing the sound and searching for a letter name representation for it: the letter name "a" or "r" for the first sound of "up." The child writes "ap" or "rp" for "up"; "cap" for "cup." These spellings are all quite deliberate choices made by young writers who are beginning to represent the sounds they hear with the letters of the alphabet.

• A letter is a word. When children start to represent written letters with sounds heard, some, but not all, focus so intently on this new discovery that they use only the first letter for each word. Previously they might have had an occasional first letter

Name: NATASHA

Things I have discovered about minibeasts

THFK(minibeasts)MEN B S A F E N P T (are) (important) (to me.)
BWN(The)GA(grasshoppers)PS K W C(can only jump with) W S(The) (the) (back) B L(legs)
aThAGHKAK O E LAPW(The)BKES
HaESOMEN B SAFAEP tto me
ThAFe FUSEYAMNE BTEN
ASthA(I don't)lot SONE(step on) (them) (or there will be) LEWNE ALON(less.)
GEBE
THAGETO(Spiders can spin a web to catch their food.)
ANT

· It is interesting to compare
work sample with "Things
About Minibeasts" dated
Natasha is now eager to
her knowledge through wri·

Things I have discovered about minibeasts (topic evaluation)
Students were asked to write down as many facts as they could about minibeasts to
inform someone who does not know anything about minibeasts. Students were also
encouraged to draw and label diagrams of various minibeasts.

Mini Beasts are important to me
Natasha

Figure 6–7

correct and with that first letter included other, space-holding letters to finish the
words. When children write one letter for a word teachers might think they have
regressed, for their writing, which contained groups of letters, is suddenly just a
string of letters. The big difference is that now each letter represents the first sound
of each word. Can you read Anthony's writing (Figure 6–8)?

Note that Anthony has spelled "bike," "BR." Why has he used letter "R"? When
asked to name the letter he had used with letter "B," Anthony replied "K" (letter
name). So at this stage he was confusing the letters "R" and "K." Thus, for this piece
of writing every letter used by Anthony represents a sound heard in his speech.
"RD" for "after" represents the way many young children pronounce the word. As
said earlier, the letter "r" is often used by young children to represent either the
sound heard at the beginning of "after" or the sound heard at the start of "up."

Anthony, age six
Rd   After
S   school
I   I
M   am
P   playing
E   in
W   water
N   and
I   I
M   am
O   going
T   to
R   ride
M   my
BR   bike

After school I am playing in water and I am going to ride my bike.

Figure 6–8

- Letters representing most or all sounds heard in each word. Here the representation of vowel sounds is evident.
- The move to conventional spelling. The writing now is easily read by others and many words are spelled automatically in conventional form. A range of spelling strategies is evident: sound-it-out, visual, morphemic, mnemonic, syllabic.

Students Learn the Subsystems of Language as They Use the Language

Learning language subsystems such as spelling (including phonics), handwriting, and punctuation, occurs as children are actually using language. It is as children use language that teachers can best observe and identify the needs of each student. Teaching to observed needs builds relevancy into the teaching/learning program. This same relevancy cannot be assured in a class where all children learn the same words or practice the same handwriting at the same time. For teachers to follow predetermined teaching sequences of spelling words, or letter/sound patterns, or letter formation, is to guarantee little, if any, benefit for many of the students in a class. Some will be practicing things they already know, while others will not understand what it is they are being made to remember. Only by teaching to observed needs as children actually use language (that is, as they read and write) will the teaching be relevant and, hence, increase the confidence and competence of the learners.

Spelling

Too much concern with correct spelling can seriously intimidate writers, who will either write little, or harangue teachers and classmates for help with spelling, or play it safe and only use those words they can spell. Extreme levels of concern with correct spelling may stop a writer from writing altogether. When this happens, the purpose in learning to spell has been lost. Spelling is for writing. Children's spelling will only improve with frequent writing and reading. It is through writing that a child has the opportunity to try out his beliefs about spelling. Of course, feedback from the teacher or some other experienced writer to the young writer is necessary to confirm current spelling knowledge or provide new information.

The process of learning to spell is developmental; it takes place over time with much experimentation on the part of the learner. When writers need words they cannot spell, they try out their beliefs about spelling. They add what they are uncertain about to what they know. Regular experiences with print give learning writers the opportunity to confirm or reject their current beliefs about the spelling and sound/letter patterns of particular words. "Learners use what they know (that is, what they believe to be true) to predict, confirm and relate new information to old" (Cochrane et al. 1984, 110).

Natasha, in her first year at school, writes about the death of her dad's dog (Figure 6–9). She read her writing as follows:

> My dad used to have a dog but his dog died. I was one when his dog died.
>
> —NATASHA

What can we say about Natasha's writing? She is able to recount a personal experience. She does not allow worry about spelling to impede her writing. Regarding her spelling, note how she has conventional spelling of some words: *my*, *Dad*, *to*, *dog*, *his*, *I*. She uses a sound-it-out spelling strategy for *used* ("yes"), *but* ("bat"), *died* ("did"), and a visual-recall strategy for the spelling of *one* ("oen"). When sounding out she uses letter names for letter sounds. In "BAT" (*but*) she uses the letter name "a," which sounds more like the middle sound of the word *but* than the letter name "u." In spelling "died" Natasha has used the letter name "i" for the middle sound of the word.

Teachers need to be able to interpret and appreciate the logic behind children's approximated spellings. Natasha's spelling of "bat" (*but*) tells me she has perfect pho-

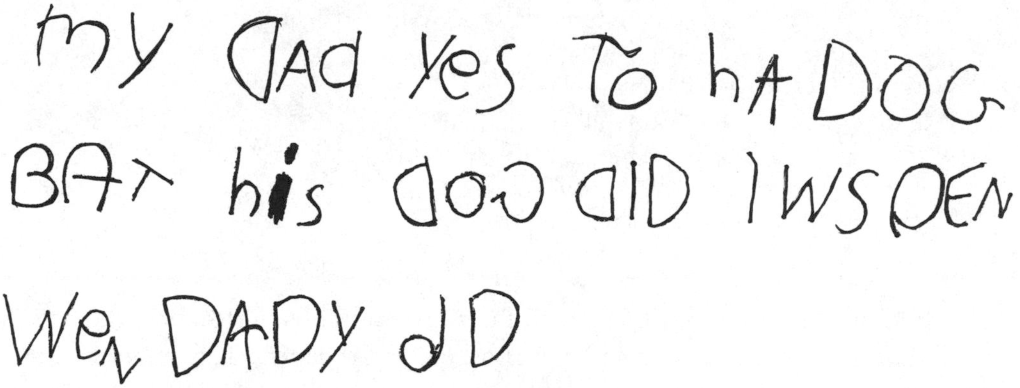

**my dad yes to ha DOG
BAt his dog did I ws pen
we dady dD**

My dad used to have a dog but his dog died. I was one when his dog died.
Natasha

Figure 6–9

nemic awareness for that word. She is hearing each of the sounds. In relation to her phonics she has two correct letter/sound representations and one approximated representation that is quite logical.

Handwriting

Ken Goodman wrote, "Whole language teachers understand that writing is not a skill that can be learned first and then used. Instruction in letter formation is built into real literacy events. Control will take a while, and development will be characterised by miscues and imperfections" (1986, 48). Thus, learning to handwrite is just part of the total writing program. It is not a prerequisite; that is, something that comes first. Rather, handwriting practice occurs when the children's writing reveals they are consciously choosing letters for particular words; they know the names of the letters and the purpose they serve. Knowing how to form letters such that they may be formed in a fluid movement is a desirable handwriting skill. That is, fluency of handwriting style is a worthy objective to work toward. However, this does not mean that all members of the same class should do the same handwriting lesson each morning of the school week.

Handwriting

First thing each morning after nine
Place our rulers straight in line,
Place red pen next to black pen neat,
Then sit up, backs against the seat.

Eyes on the teacher, she's watching you.
Don't talk unless requested to.
"Now everybody write the date

Then copy the handwriting. Keep it straight.
Start each letter at the top.
For letter 'i' do add the dot."

Thirty hands all write in time.
Thirty children tow the line.
Thirty spirits slowly broken.
Thirty robots in the makin'.

—LORRAINE WILSON

When children start both to use letters in their early writing and to know the names of the letters, it is meaningful to instruct about letter formation. This might be done individually after a conference with a child; for example, if the teacher notices a letter that is not formed well she might write it at the bottom of the child's paper, talk about the starting point, and ask the child to practice forming the letter several times. Alternatively, the teacher may give handwriting instruction to a small group of children who have similar handwriting needs. It is advantageous for fluency in continuous writing that children start the formation of letters in positions that allow the hand to continue fluidly onto the next letter, hence the value of showing children correct starting points when writing script print in the early years of schooling.

As with learning to spell, the children are encouraged to look for patterns of similarity and difference in the formation of the letters. It makes good sense to practice handwriting a group of letters with a similar element or starting position.

Handwriting and Audience
Development of a legible writing style is linked with the purpose and audience for writing. There are occasions when it is necessary, courteous, or politically expedient to write neatly, fluently, and legibly. Sometimes parents become concerned when they see that young writers are allowed to scribble or write in unreadable ways in what are called writing books. It is diplomatic to include in the child's cumulative assessment file samples of writing that show that the school program values the development of a legible handwriting style. The child's cumulative evaluation file should show the child's ongoing ability to handwrite differently in different contexts (e.g., drafting, writing the final copy of a letter, hand lettering the cover of a book).

Classroom Practice
The class work described here exemplifies issues discussed throughout the chapter.

Integrating Listening, Speaking, Reading, and Writing
Leanne Schulz and her grade 2–3 children undertook an integrated study of animals and their environments. A focus of the study was the threat of extinction to some living

species brought about by the interaction of humans with the environment. I share with you several lessons that occurred near the end of the study.

The children listened as Leanne read aloud from *Where Would We Sleep? Children on the Environment* (Temple 1992). This book is a collection of letters written by children from many different countries to the world. In the letters the children address their wishes for the future for the world.

The children formed pairs and copies of different letters from the book were given to each pair (one letter per two children). The children read and discussed the issues raised in the letters.

In a following session, each pair of children prepared their letter for presentation to the whole grade, by Readers Theatre. They read the letter aloud together, after which they discussed how the letter may be broken into parts for a group presentation. They practiced reading the letter in parts, and finally, shared their presentation with the whole class.

The children then individually drafted a letter to the world about his or her hope for the future in relation to the natural environment. After conferencing with the teacher, the letters were redrafted and later published as a class collection, which was available for all the children to read. Note Jasper's heartfelt letter.

> *Dear World,*
>
> *I have some friends. I'd like to see me and my friends hiking up a mountain watching the sunset go down . . . down . . . down. Then I think of the stars blacked out by lots and lots and lots of factories, endless fumes of smoke covering them. I feel sad. Bits of my heart are falling off. When that happens I think about my kitten Bronsin and that makes me cry. I hope the world lives forever*
>
> *From your friend*
>
> *Jasper, age eight*

Note how this integrated learning involved the children listening, speaking, reading, and writing.

Immersions and Demonstrations

Demonstrating the Writing of a Particular Text Form   I was working in a K–2 classroom on writing nonrhyming poetry. Each session began with immersions in the text form. Poems were displayed in large print as they were read aloud. Each session also began with me demonstrating how I write poetry. On one occasion, I recounted to the children a quite frightening experience of the previous evening. While at home alone and upstairs, a picture fell off the wall in the downstairs living room. The sound of breaking glass caused me to fear that someone was breaking in.

Over several sessions I drafted the following poem about the incident. Here is draft four.

Shattered Evening

One evening
As I prepared for bed
The smash of glass breaking
Broke the quiet
And paralysing fear
Immobilised me.

I listened
Hardly daring to breathe.
No further sounds of trespass.

Gathering courage
I crept downstairs
Expecting a broken door panel
Or smashed window.
Shattered glass across the carpet
Revealed
A picture had fallen off the wall.

As usual, I asked the children for their comments. The children were accustomed to my referring to some conference questions relating to the writing of poetry, one of which was "Have I used the best words?" It was not surprising, then, when one seven-year-old challenged "quiet" as the best word. He thought I should try "silence." I read the poem aloud using "silence" instead of "quiet" in line 4. The children and I generally agreed that "silence" sounded better. I made the change. A second young learner then suggested that he didn't think I should keep the word "revealed." Note the influence here of earlier demonstrations of mine where I asked myself, "Do I need all the words?" I read the poem aloud in its entirety, changing the word "quiet" to "silence" and omitting "revealed," and pausing after "carpet," before continuing with the final line. I was very happy with this revision. The poem now reads

Shattered Evening

One evening
As I prepared for bed
The smash of glass breaking
Broke the silence
And paralysing fear
Immobilised me.

I listened
Hardly daring to breathe.
No further sounds of trespass

So
Gathering courage
I crept downstairs
Expecting a broken door panel
Or smashed window.

Shattered glass across the carpet—
A picture had fallen off the wall.

—LORRAINE WILSON

After such demonstrations, I observe the young writers as they emulate what they have observed—being fussy with word choices and deleting unnecessary words.

Learning the Subsystems of Language in Context

Proofreading for Punctuation   When, with permission, a student's draft writing is written out large enough for all to see, editing the piece for punctuation or for spelling with other students observing can be a focused teaching for the whole class.

Hien is learning English as a second language. Her finished draft revealed that she understood how to use quotation marks before and after direct speech but was not aware of the need for a capital letter. This is an extract from her draft.

"take it home" and then I said " alright" the next day my brother said "sell it for money" and I said "no because I can do something really good with this that's why I don't want to sell it" "alright then" he said. Then I said to my friend "can I borrow your car?" and he said "why?" I said "I'm going to drag people" and he said "can I come."

—HIEN, GRADE 5–6

I copied this extract of her draft in large letters and, with her permission displayed it at the start of a writing session. As usual, the children were reminded that this shared demonstration time using actual student writing was a time to be supportive of one another and to offer constructive assistance. Before focusing on the direct speech we did spend some time with Hien rereading and considering where some full stops might assist the reader.

Next, the children were asked to silently read the draft and think where capital letters might be inserted. Hien did this too, and, when ready, she commenced marking the capital letters on her draft with the other children observing. Here is the same piece of writing with the changes she made while her classmates watched.

"Take it home." Then I said "Alright." The next day my brother said "Sell it for money" I said "No because I can do something really cool with this that's why I don't want to sell it." "Alright then" he said. Then I said to my friend "Can I borrow your car?" and he said "Why?" I said "I'm going to drag people" and he said "can I come?"

When the student finishes making corrections, classmates often suggest other issues to attend to. Although Hien has much to learn about writing in English, this proofreading activity was focused learning for her.

Word Sorting for Spelling Patterns   Known words—that is, words children can read and pronounce—are a very good resource for investigating spelling patterns. These words might be the children's names or words from an integrated unit of study.

Sorts can be open or closed. In open sorts, children sort according to their own categories. The children might sort the words into same first-letter groups; words with double letters and words without double letters; groups of words with common sounds; words formed from the same base word; compound words; or words with the same number of syllables.

Children must articulate the criteria for group membership of words. Allowing children to sort according to their own criteria provides evidence of their knowledge about words and about the different spelling strategies they use when writing. Children from Vicki McCormack and Helen Lockart's K–2 class sorted words from a friendship list into groups of their own choosing. They had to write reasons for group membership. Here are some of their groupings.

double letters	all have ing (sound)	they all have "en"
manners	helping	friends
feelings	giving	friendly
funny	caring	friendship
happiness	loving	
cheerful	feelings	
happy	including	
letter	pleasing	

all of them have "a"
pen pal
sharing
share

the word "friend" is in all of them	the word "help" is in them	caring
friends	help	happiness
friendship	helpful	happy
friendly	helping	considerate
		thankful
		special

"g" words	four letter words	pleasing
good	nice	grateful
great	kind	
giving	like	
grateful	good	

one syllable words	two syllables
great	friendship
good	friendly
strong	helpful
sweet	sharing
kind	feelings
nice	helping
like	happy
smart	loving
	thankful

These are just some of the groupings the children devised. Note how they have grouped according to sound/letter pattern (ing), letter sequence (en), double letters, number of letters, number of syllables, base words (friends, friendly, friendship).

In closed sorts, children sort to given criterion. For example, find all the words in which you hear the "o" sound (as in middle of "cot"); find all the compound words.

Summary

For writers to be able and willing to write for justice, they need to feel confident as writers. Classroom learning programs can make or break learners' belief in themselves. A class program that begins for each individual with his existing understandings; that integrates the development of listening, speaking, reading, and writing; that immerses the learners in an extensive print environment; that includes demonstrations of different aspects of writing authentically; that encourages risk taking and experimentation; and that implements explicit teaching of the subsystems of language in the context of the language being used has great potential to build such writers.

References

Cambourne, B. 1988. *The Whole Story: Natural Learning and the Acquisiton of Literacy*. Auckland: Ashton Scholastic.

Christensen, L. 2000. *Reading, Writing and Rising Up*. Milwaukee, MN: A Rethinking Schools Publication.

Cochrane, O., D. Cochrane, S. Scalena, and E. Buchanan. 1984. *Reading, Writing and Caring*. Winnipeg: Whole Language Consultants.

Goodman, K. 1986. *What's Whole in Whole Language*. Ontario, Canada: Scholastic.

Smith, F. 1984. "The Creative Achievement of Literacy." In *Awakening to Literacy*, edited by H. Goelman, A. Oberg, and F. Smith. London: Heinemann Educational Books.

Woodward, V. A., J. C. Harste, and C. L. Burke. 1984. *Language Stories and Literacy Lessons*. Portsmouth, NH: Heinemann.

Children's Book

Temple, L. 1992. *Where Would We Sleep? Children on the Environment*. Sydney, Australia: Random House.

CHAPTER 7

WORKING TOWARD A DEMOCRATIC CLASSROOM

It is the start of a new school year. I arrange with teacher friends Jan Hayes, Leanne Schulz, Annie Drennan, and Shirl Ramage, who team teach two grade 5–6 units, to work together toward developing democratic classrooms. These teachers and their students have a long history of working in democratic ways. Their school has an equal-opportunity policy and the student welfare and discipline policy includes each grade formulating their agreed rights, responsibilities, and consequences anew each year. Cooperative learning is employed in all classrooms. Each class votes for a student representative for the Student Representative Council, which is the student voice to the governing school board. But we have never before used the word "democratic" when speaking with the students about their classrooms. This year we determined to focus on democratic ways of living, not only in the classroom, but also in the local community and the wider world. Of course, classroom communities exist within school communities, which in turn exist within system communities, so there is legislation, and there are required operating procedures, which form boundaries and restraints and which impact the structure and activity of democratic classroom communities for both teachers and students.

Activities for Democratic Classrooms

Listed below are some actual class activities in which we engage children in the first month of the school year. Some of these activities are initiated by Jan, Leanne, Shirl, and Annie.

Tapping Existing Knowledge: Defining "Democratic"

Individually, the children write their responses to the question What does it mean to live and work together democratically? It is interesting that the introduction of the word "democratic" seems to throw some children, who find it difficult to get more than a sentence on their paper, while others are more comfortable using their knowledge to venture lengthier answers (Figures 7–1, 7–2, and 7–3).

I think it means too work
and live together in peace
I havn't heard of the word
but I'e heard of similair ones
I also belive that it might
mean to obey laws and rights.

In the classroom it might mean
for everyone to have a fair
say, everyone to share and
work co-optervely.

Figure 7–1   Callum

I think "Democratic" means like a communion,
and to be in it you have to work together
and follow the rules, and stand strong.
Everyone has to be involved. But everyone has to have
a say.

Figure 7–2   Sam

I think it means that you live and work together fairly. You know
how to work together, and you know everybodys everyones
rights and you dont abuse them. If you have to decide
something you do it fairly maybe by voting. So you a kind
of do everything professienly and what the majority thinks
goes.

Figure 7–3   Sophia

Valuing Selves: Developing Self-Awareness, and Self-Pride

On the first day of school, each student writes a letter to his or her teacher explaining why that teacher is lucky to have that student in her class. The letters are displayed around the classroom with self-portraits. (Figures 7–4, 7–5, 7–6, and 7–7).

Another activity to promote self-pride is a reading of *Skin Again*, by bell hooks. This picture storybook invites readers to look beyond skin color and find the treasures stored

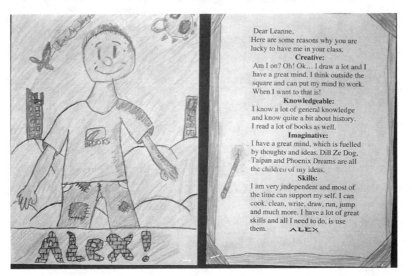

Figure 7–4   Alex

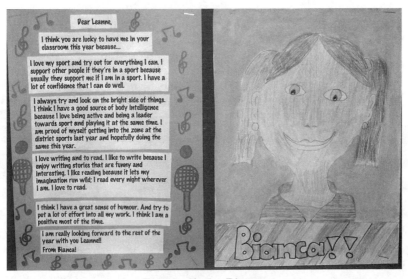

Figure 7–5   Bianca

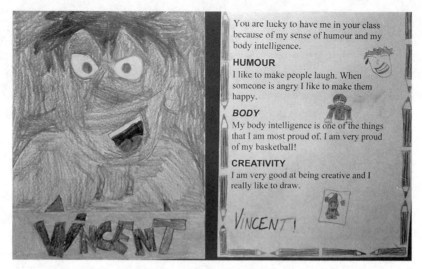

Figure 7–6   Vincent

beneath. It invites new ways to talk about race and identity. We begin by reading *Skin Again* aloud. We ask the children to think about their skin; their outward appearance, and then to think about who they are beneath their skin, what they feel inside. The book is read aloud a second time, and the children are asked to use art media to illustrate their inner selves (Figures 7–8, 7–9, and 7–10).

Valuing Difference

For this activity, the children first share their artistic representations of their inner selves, triggered by listening to *Skin Again*, in small groups. Then each child is asked to find a

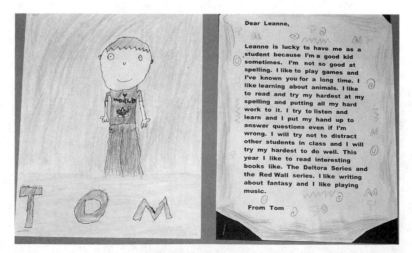

Figure 7–7   Tom

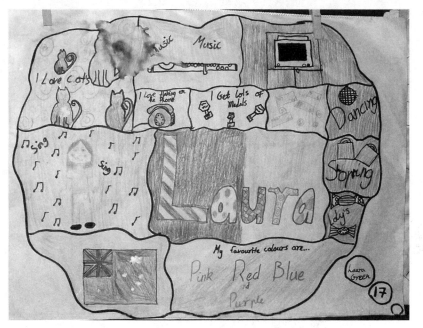

Figure 7–8   Laura

Figure 7–9   Camilla

Figure 7–10   Bianca

child they do not know well and to share what they have created. This helps students get to know new classmates and each other. A whole-class share follows. The children are prompted, "In class we are investigating what it means to live and work together democratically. Why then have we asked you to reveal who you are on the inside?" Points the children make include:

> You want to get to know us.
>
> It shows we are not the same.
>
> It helps us get to know one another.
>
> It shows there are differences between us.
>
> It's okay to be different.

Cooperating and Compromising
Cat and Fish, a picture storybook by Joan Grant, tells of the meeting between a cat and a fish. They come from different worlds but like one another and learn to compromise so they can live together.

Cat and Fish is read aloud while the children listen and enjoy. The book is read a second time, and this time the children listen and focus on any underlying message the author may be giving. The children then write what they perceive the author's message(s) to be (Figures 7–11, 7–12, and 7–13).

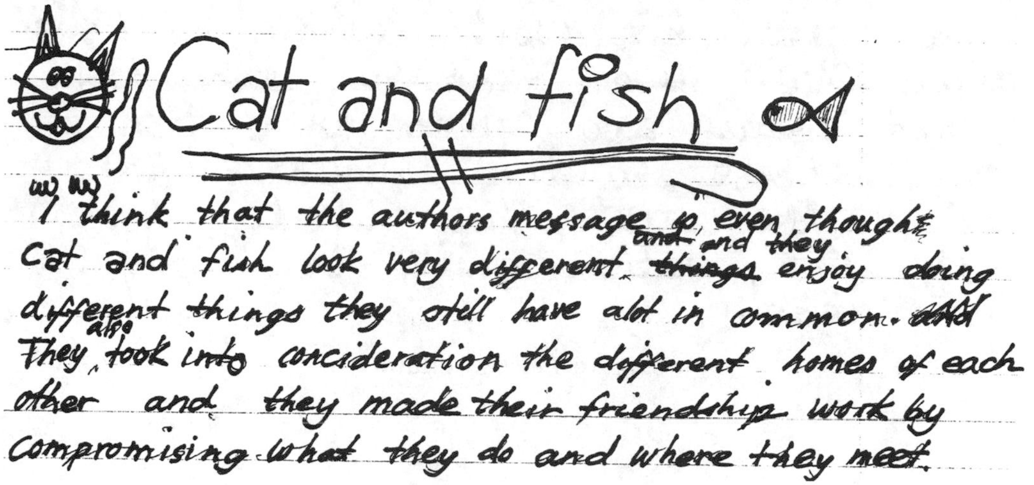

Cat and fish

I think that the authors message is, even though Cat and fish look very different things and and they enjoy doing different things they still have alot in common. also They took into concideration the different homes of each other and they made their friendship work by compromising what they do and where they meet.

Figure 7–11   Sophia

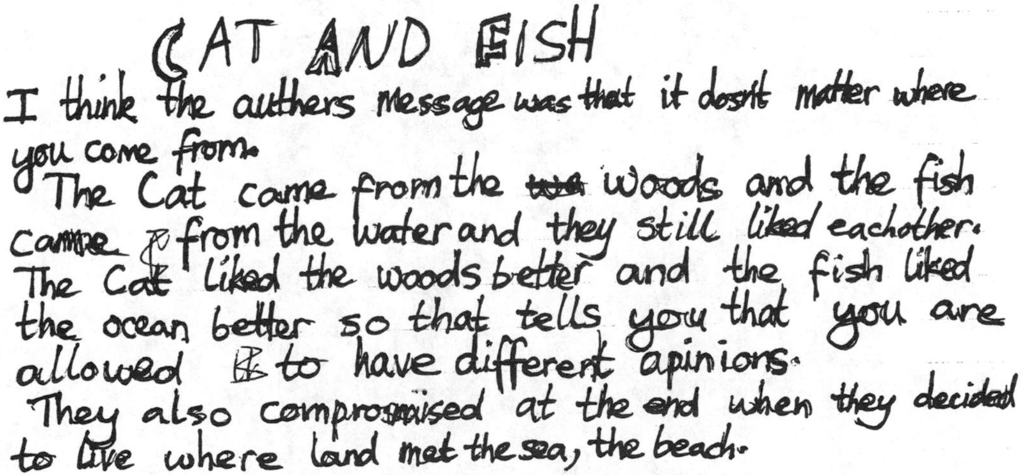

CAT AND FISH

I think the authers message was that it dosn't matter where you come from.
The Cat came from the woods and the fish came from the water and they still liked eachother.
The Cat liked the woods better and the fish liked the ocean better so that tells you that you are allowed to have different apinions.
They also compromised at the end when they decided to live where land met the sea, the beach.

Figure 7–12   Ben

We gather together on the carpet in groups of three or four, and the children share their messages. Individual children then nominate others from their group to share with the whole group. A class list of author messages is compiled (Figure 7–14). We take

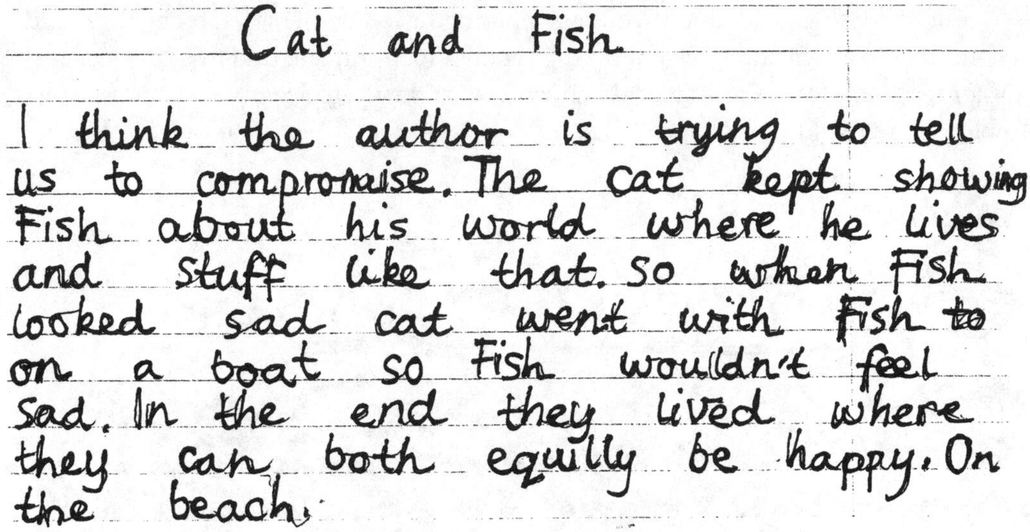

Cat and Fish

I think the author is trying to tell us to compromise. The cat kept showing Fish about his world where he lives and stuff like that. So when Fish looked sad cat went with Fish to on a boat so Fish wouldn't feel sad. In the end they lived where they can both equilly be happy. On the beach.

Figure 7–13   Callum

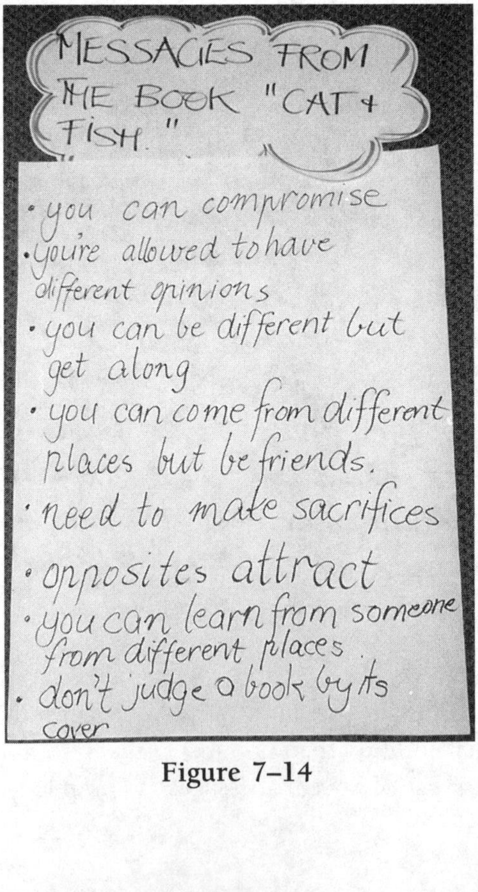

MESSAGES FROM THE BOOK "CAT & FISH."

- you can compromise
- you're allowed to have different opinions
- you can be different but get along
- you can come from different places but be friends.
- need to make sacrifices
- opposites attract
- you can learn from someone from different places.
- don't judge a book by its cover

Figure 7–14

time to dicuss how readers may interpret the same literary text differently; different readers do not always perceive the same underlying message, yet each person's interpretation is valid.

Next, the children are asked to apply or relate the author's messages to their own worlds at home, at school, or even in the wider world. They write about a situation where these ideas applied (Figures 7–15, 7–16, and 7–17).

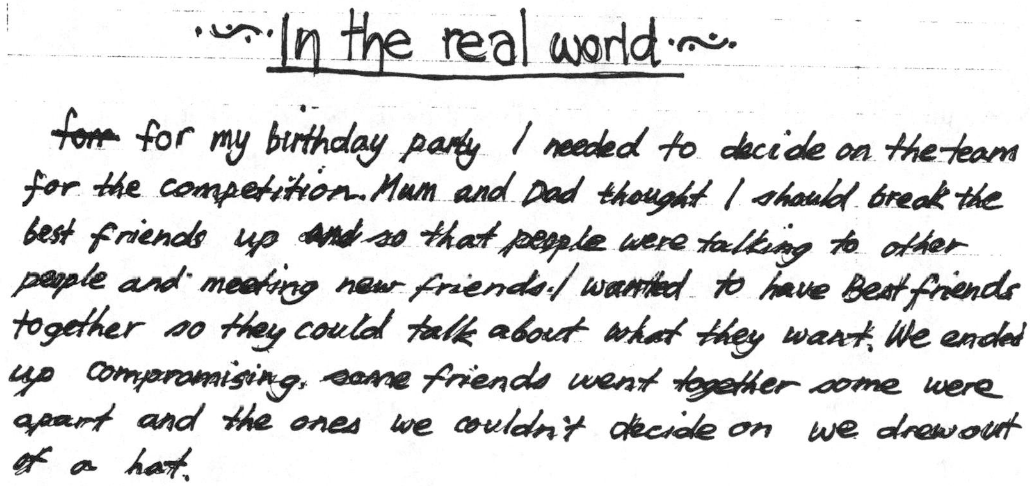

⸱⸱In the real world⸱⸱

~~fore~~ for my birthday party I needed to decide on the team for the competition. Mum and Dad thought I should break the best friends up ~~and so~~ that people were talking to other people and meeting new friends. I wanted to have Best friends together so they could talk about what they want. We ended up compromising. ~~some~~ friends went together some were apart and the ones we couldn't decide on we drew out of a hat.

Figure 7–15   Sophia

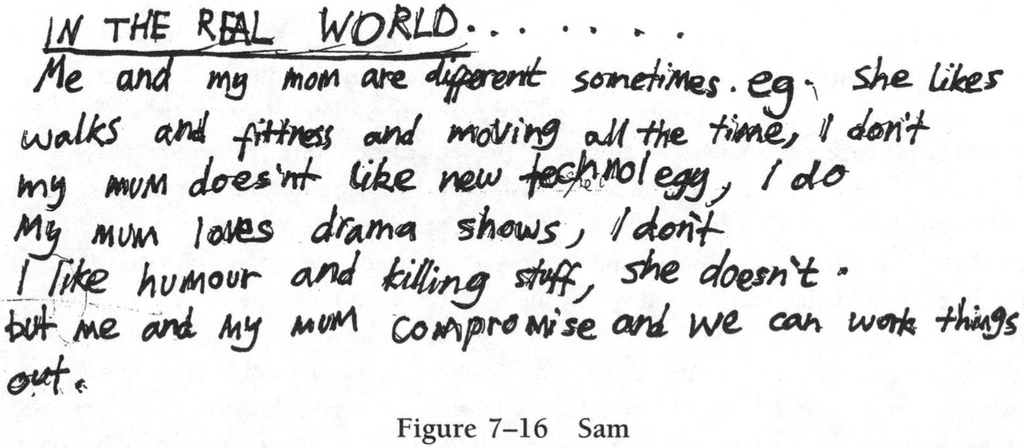

IN THE REAL WORLD. . . . . .

Me and my mom are different sometimes. eg. she likes walks and fittness and moving all the time, I don't
my mum does'nt like new technology, I do
My mum loves drama shows, I don't
I like humour and killing stuff, she doesn't .
but me and my mum compromise and we can work things out.

Figure 7–16   Sam

When I was playing indoor soccer Ben and I both wanted to take the penalty so we compromised and said you take the first penalty and I'll take the next penalty

Figure 7–17   Callum

Language for Living Democratically

Vocabulary   The children are asked to think of particular words that people use as part of living and working together democratically. A class list is compiled:

democracy	democratic	democratically
justice	fair	participation
respect	compromise	compromising
sacrificing	differences	help
fair	vote	power
listen	negotiate	reasoning
rules	rights	acceptance
responsibilities	consequences	consideration
share	help	communion
different	discuss	contributing
similar	contribute	voice
choices	caring	election
resolution		

Sentence Construction   The children are asked to think about the language of discussion. Are there particular ways of beginning sentences that invite contributions from others? Can language be used to thwart or prevent discussion?

The children divide into pairs, with one child playing a parent and one a child. Each pair discusses what they will do that afternoon. They then develop two role-plays: the first where the parent is dominant and the child gets no say; the second where a decision is reached democratically. Ask the children to notice how they use language. Does the language change in the two role-plays? If so, how?

Some of the role-plays are shared. Then we jointly list ways of beginning sentences that are inclusive and invite contributions, and ways that are overbearing, domineering, and prevent joint decision making. Here the children are actually noticing the modality of language—the certainty or possibilities that language evokes. Compare "We will all go on a picnic this afternoon" with "Perhaps we could have a picnic this afternoon."

Next, the children write the two role-plays in which they engaged, noticing how the language differs in each, particularly the sentence beginnings (Figure 7–18).

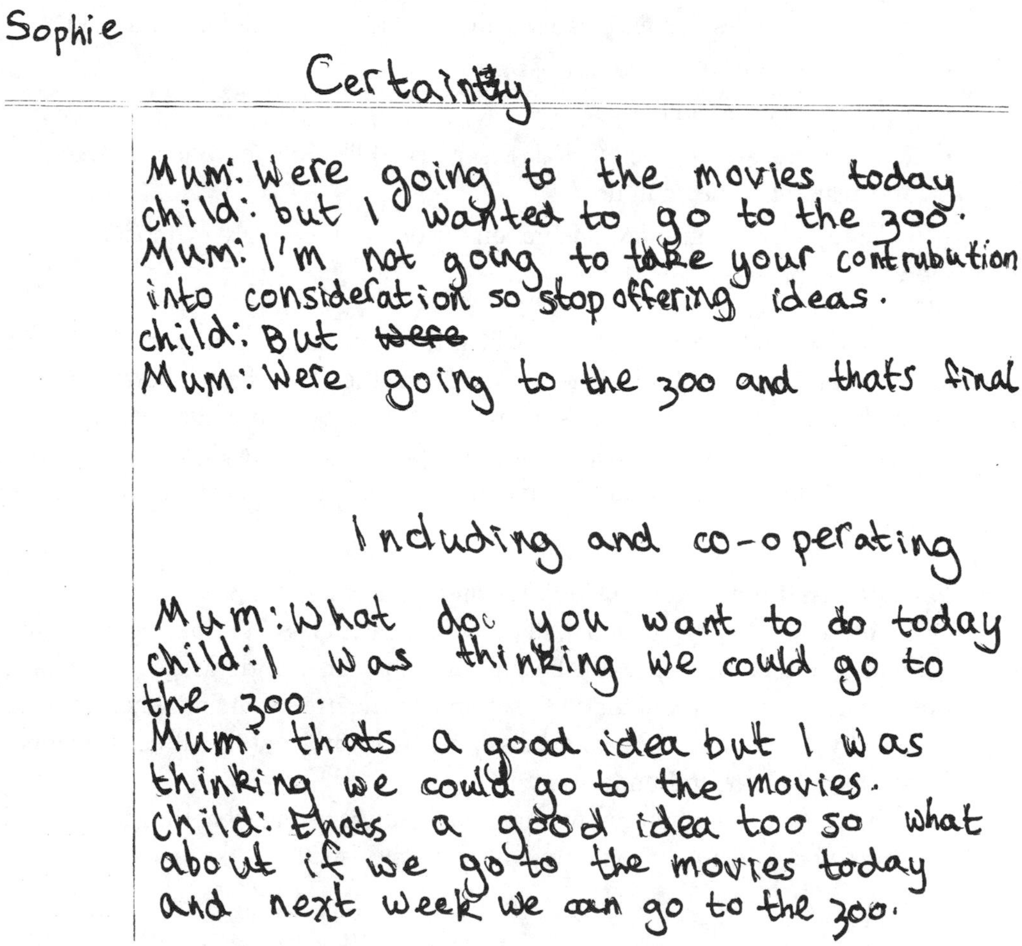

Sophie

Certainty

Mum: Were going to the movies today
child: but I wanted to go to the zoo.
Mum: I'm not going to take your contrubution into consideration so stop offering ideas.
child: But ~~were~~
Mum: Were going to the zoo and thats final

Including and co-operating

Mum: What do you want to do today
child: I was thinking we could go to the zoo.
Mum: thats a good idea but I was thinking we could go to the movies.
child: thats a good idea too so what about if we go to the movies today and next week we can go to the zoo.

Figure 7–18

In the next session, we build on the teaching described above. In a small group of three, we, the teachers, role-play both democratic and undemocratic decision making in a discussion related to preparing a special celebratory staff lunch. We want the children to see how we role-play by speaking, not acting, and to listen particularly for how we start our sentences.

Following our demonstration, the children work in groups of four. Each role-play is done twice; first with one group member being very dictatorial, the second with group members coming to a decision cooperatively and democratically. Group members may either be friends of the same age, or have adults and children. Here is the list of possible scenarios.

Living and Working Together Democratically
- You discuss the choice of a film for Saturday afternoon.
- A family (includes a parent) discusses the purchase of new clothes for a child.
- Four classmates plan a joint class activity.
- A family plans a holiday.
- Four friends are together at Walt Disney World®. They have just arrived and plan what they will do.
- A family plans a birthday celebration for one of the family members.
- A child's bedroom is to be redecorated.

Some groups share their role-plays, after which the role-players comment on some of their sentence beginnings. More entries are made on the class chart. The children are now noticing that some words are less definite and more inviting, like "perhaps," and "maybe." They notice also that inviting language poses more questions: "What would you think . . ."; "How about . . ." In the undemocratic language of exclusion, questions are not evident.

Developing Class Rights, Responsibilities, and Consequences
As part of the school discipline and welfare policy, each class develops agreed rights, responsibilities, and consequences at the start of each year. The rights, responsibilities, and consequences are displayed for all to see and are referred to if and when someone transgresses. In other words, classroom discipline is formulated by all class members and is open for all to see and understand.

Even the youngest children can work in small groups listing what they believe their school rights to be. Often they come up with examples such as

> not to be hit
> not to be bullied
> not to be teased

After the initial brainstorming of what the children believe their rights to be, they take part in grouping the rights they have listed; for example, they may combine the examples above to read "to feel safe." The following list is displayed in Annie and Shirl's Grade 5–6 classroom:

A right is
- something you're allowed to do within the rules;
- a privilege.

Children have the right to
- have fun at school;
- be respected and treated well at school;
- feel safe and not be bullied;
- learn without people distracting them, ask questions, and give their opinions.

Teachers have the right to
- be respected and treated well by both children and parents;
- be listened to;
- give appropriate consequences.

Parents have the right to
- expect that their child is safe at school;
- know what is going on at school and express their feelings and concerns about school.

A responsibility is
- related to a right; you have responsibilities when you have a right;
- taking care of your own actions;
- something you are expected to do; if you aren't responsible, there may be consequences.

Behaviors displayed when acting responsibly include
- treating others well, like you want to be treated (no bullying);
- caring for people;
- staying on task, meeting deadlines, concentrating, paying attention;
- being punctual;
- playing safely;
- trusting people;
- looking after school equipment;
- being a positive role model;
- working well in groups;
- respecting other people's work and belongings.

A consequence is
- a fair punishment for when you haven't been responsible;
- something you should expect and accept if you've done something wrong;
- related to rights and responsibilities;

- something you get if you don't act responsibly and you may lose your right;
- something you can learn from.

In the classroom, the words "right," "responsibility," and "consequence" are very much part of the classroom vocabulary. If someone transgresses, there are open discussions about what has happened; which right has been infringed, and what an appropriate consequence might be. The children often help formulate appropriate consequences.

What Does It Mean to Live and Work Together Democratically?

Children return to a task given them at the start of this work. Later, a class list is compiled.

Living and working together democratically means we
- vote
- no-one dominating
- share together
- compromise
- letting other people have opinions
- deciding as a group
- make everyone equal in a conversation
- don't judge people
- let everyone have a choice
- don't cut people off when they're talking

—Ben

Living and working together democratically means we
- compromise
- vote/have elections
- share opinions ideas
- don't block out people
- communicate together
- co-operate
- don't dominate
- make decisions together
- have rights and responsibilities
- have consequences
- are fair to everyone

—Jess

This work is ongoing. At the time of this writing, the children are investigating the concept of power. They are describing situations in their own lives where they feel powerful, and powerless (Figure 7–19) (Murdoch and Hamston 1999, 158). As the year

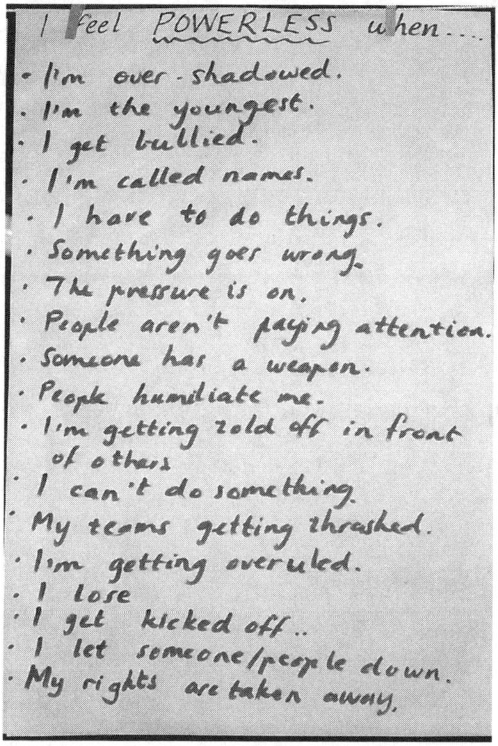

> I feel POWERLESS when....
> - I'm over-shadowed.
> - I'm the youngest.
> - I get bullied.
> - I'm called names.
> - I have to do things.
> - Something goes wrong.
> - The pressure is on.
> - People aren't paying attention.
> - Someone has a weapon.
> - People humiliate me.
> - I'm getting told off in front of others
> - I can't do something.
> - My teams getting thrashed.
> - I'm getting overuled.
> - I lose
> - I get kicked off..
> - I let someone/people down.
> - My rights are taken away.

Figure 7–19   Class List Showing When Leanne's Students Feel Powerless

progresses the class lists will continue to be referred to and revised. The children will be encouraged to apply principles of democratic living, not only in their classrooms but also in the schoolyard and at home. The following class list reveals the need for children to continue to challenge each other's understandings and to classify and group their statements in an effort to identify the key concepts that underpin democracy.

Living and Working Together Democratically Means We

- share
- listen to/accept opinions
- compromise and make sacrifices
- ask instead of telling
- let other people's ideas be heard
- include people
- have rights, responsibilities, and consequences
- discuss
- vote for a decision when necessary
- are fair

- have a say
- go by the rules
- aren't afraid to ask and express our point of view
- make sure the majority are happy with decisions
- have equal power within our groups/treat each other equally
- find ways to resolve issues in nonviolent ways
- able to make choices
- cooperate
- communicate respectfully with each other
- accept/respect other people and their differences
- try to understand each other
- work together
- take/give time to make decisions
- do not dominate in arguments
- put differences aside
- care about issues that are life-threatening
- all have a voice for what counts
- are not afraid to speak in front of others

Principles for the Development of Democratic Classrooms

Certain principles underlie the development of democratic classrooms. Without them educating children to right the world becomes a hit-or-miss affair (Emmitt and Wilson 2005).

- Each member of the community is valued.

  Value does not vary with race, religion, nationality, gender, or academic or physical ability.

  The curriculum is designed to enable all students to learn.
- Members know themselves (who they are; what they value) and work to know and understand other members.

  Members of a group do not need to be the same to live together harmoniously and democratically.
- Agreed rules and punishments are formulated by group members.

  Classroom rules may take the form of rights, responsibilities, and consequences.

  The group's rights, rules, and punishments are visible and familiar to all members.
- School-based curriculum decision making is valued by the wider education system.

- Decision making is negotiated within the boundaries of system constraints and the class rules.

     Children and teachers can negotiate topics or subtopics for investigation, time commitments, etc.

- The functioning of democratic communities requires particular language use.

     Vocabulary: value, worth, justice, fairness, difference, similarities, compromise, negotiate, taking turns, accommodate, share, respect, rights, responsibilities, consequences, rules, government, voting, majority, etc.

     Modality: "Perhaps we might consider . . ." versus "We should do . . ."; "What would you think of . . ." versus "The best and only course of action is . . ."

     Dialect: Children's language is accepted by teachers; no child is put down because of the way he or she speaks.

- Critical literacy is necessary for the maintenance of democratic ways of being.

     to detect stereotypes in texts

     to determine the values and purposes of authors

     to determine whether to accept or reject a particular author's constructions of social groups

     to be willing and able to take action against prejudiced, biased texts.

Summary: Democratic Classrooms

If our worldview is one where people work together to establish a more equitable and just society for all peoples, then young children (our future citizens) must experience democracy at work as they live and grow, ideally both at home and at school, but certainly at school. The values we hope our students will take out into their worlds must be lived in their classrooms. They should be members of classrooms that are democratic communities. Members of democratic communities feel valued; experience respect from other members; show respect to classmates; know their rights and responsibilities and the consequences for the infringement of these rights; and feel they have a voice in the running of the community. Members of democratic communities are free to be different while respecting the rights and differences of others. They learn ways of negotiating and compromising to avoid conflict.

> As I write previously, classroom management and children's classroom behaviour are intimately connected to democracy. Democracy at its best involves people living together in familial, local, national and global communities . . . By helping our students explore issues of our in-school and out-of-school behaviour, we are teaching and learning about much more than just behaviour, we are shaping our entire beings and helping kids create who they want to be and how they want to live as members of those democratic communities. At its best the classroom becomes the life itself. We no longer teach about democracy and community, but live democracy and community. (Wolk 2002, 9–10)

References

Emmitt, M., and L. Wilson. 2005. Living Democracy in the Classroom. Paper presented at the Literacies for All Summer Institute, San Diego.

Murdoch, K., and J. Hamston. 1999. *Knowing Me Knowing You*. Melbourne: Dellasta Pty Ltd.

Wolk, S. 2002. *Being Good: Rethinking Classroom Management and Student Discipline*. Portsmouth, NH: Heinemann.

Children's Books

Grant, J. 2003. *Cat and Fish*. Melbourne: Lothian Books.

hooks, b. 2004. *Skin Again*. New York: Hyperion Books for Children.

APPENDIX:
HOLISTIC BELIEF STATEMENTS

All practice described in this book is informed by the following belief statements.*

BELIEF STATEMENTS

Belief About a World View

1. A society of participatory democracy and social justice for all is dependent on school systems valuing the lives of all students irrespective of their culture, language, social class, or physical and emotional abilities; systems where individual schools and classrooms function as democratic communities and where curriculum starts with the children in those classrooms, not with state-mandated documents; systems where social critical literacy is the goal for all.

Beliefs About Language

2. Listening, speaking, reading, and writing are social practices. They are not ends in themselves. They occur as part of life activities that are purposeful and meaningful. It follows that language learning occurs best in meaningful, authentic contexts. Technological change has meant, today, that there is not one literacy but multiple literacies, all of which accompany and are part of life activities.

3. Listening, speaking, reading, and writing are not isolated, separate domains. The four language modes are interactive in the process of constructing meaning.

4. Because language (and literacy) is social practice, it changes in different social contexts. As the context changes so does the language. What is appropriate language in one context differs from what is appropriate in another. What is appropriate is shaped by the participants and the purpose for the social activity.

---

* I acknowledge the Australian TAWL Executive Committee, 1995, for the original of draft these philosophical belief statements. The statements were redrafted and updated by members of the Whole Language Umbrella at the 2002 Town Meeting, Bethesda, MD. My colleague Marie Emmitt and I have done a little tweaking to produce this current format. They can also be found at www.ncte.org/groups /wlu/who/107138.htm.

Beliefs About Learning Language

5. Students learn language and they learn about language as they use language to learn about themselves and the wider world.

6. Language is learned through interaction with other language users. These interactions include immersions in and demonstrations of language in use by more experienced language users.

7. Language learning is an active process. From their experiences with language, students formulate hypotheses about how language works. They try out their hypotheses while actually using language. These hypotheses may be approximations of language in use and are refined over time to conventional usage with further language experience, including use, immersions, demonstrations, and responses from other language users.

8. Students learn the subsystems of a language (such as spelling, syntax, and punctuation) as they engage in using language. It is as students learn language that teachers can best observe the language needs of individual learners and plan for their ongoing learning of language and of the subsystems.

Belief About Assessment

9. Assessment is essential to the teaching and learning process; it grows out of and informs instruction by recognizing the individual strengths and needs of all students.

Belief About Teachers

10. Teachers are professionals who continue to learn and who take responsibility for their own learning. They are able to articulate their beliefs and are sufficiently knowledgeable about teaching and learning to make informed curriculum decisions in planning programs for the students they teach.